Alive AF

One Anxious Mom's Journey to Becoming Alcohol Free

Samantha Perkins

Copyright 2020. All rights reserved. No part of this publication can be reproduced or transmitted in any form by any means, electronic or mechanical, without permission in writing from the author.

This work is non-fiction and, as such, reflects the author's memory of her experiences. Many of the names and identifying characteristics of the individuals featured in this book have been changed to protect their privacy and certain individuals are composites. Dialogue and events have been recreated; in some cases, conversations have been edited to convey their substance rather than written exactly as they occurred.

Paperback ISBN: 13 978-1-7362409-0-8

Ebook ISBN-13: 978-1-7364209-1-5

Cover design by onegraphica.com

 Created with Vellum

Table Of Contents

Chapter 1 Oh, Not Again!
Chapter 2 Growing Up Anxious
Chapter 3 My First Hangovers
Chapter 4 Meeting My Drinking Buddy
Chapter 5 Hangovers for Adults
Chapter 6 This is Living?
Chapter 7 Drinking To Cope
Chapter 8 Thank God for Other People's Hangovers
Chapter 9 No Thank You Please
Chapter 10 A Writer Emerges
Chapter 11 Alive AF
Conclusion
References
Acknowledgments
About The Author

For Buggy and Sister

Introduction

I once took a hangover pill. This was many years ago, before I stopped drinking. It wasn't like a Tylenol or an Alka Seltzer, but the kind of pill you take before you get a hangover. The kind that you take in preparation for over drinking. I was going to a wedding, followed by a reception. The type of event that brings up a lot of joy but also some anxiety. Who will I see? Will my ex be there? Will I have to talk to people I don't know? What am I doing with my life? The pill was to be ingested before you even start drinking to stave off the pain and suffering that would otherwise follow. I'm sure it was packed with some kind of antioxidants. I can't remember exactly, but it was sure to have had kale, pomegranate, essential oils, bear claw, hair of a wild meerkat and healing fairy dust. Otherwise I wouldn't have taken it. I did my research when it came to health and wellness and I knew how to handle hangovers.

I did other things too. I would take Tylenol before bed (after drinking). I would wake up and swish coconut oil and take an Epsom salt bath. I drank lots of water and ate a BRAT diet (banana, rice, applesauce and toast) when things were really bad. I read articles from wellness blogs about the best foods to eat for hangovers. They were titled things like "The 6 Best Hangover Cures, Backed By Science" or (the ones that really spoke to me) "Natural Hangover Cures." I changed my drinking too. I switched from dark and heavy beers to gin and water because hydration was key to staying healthy. I added lime because it has some essential nutrients.

Health was important to me. I led a life of wellness. My debilitating anxiety required a lot of care. It wasn't enough just to take meds. I needed to work out, get plenty of sleep, eat healthy and make sure that I tried to cope with hangovers appropriately. So that things didn't get too out of control. I knew what it took to care for my mental health and it wasn't easy. It required planning and preparation, hence the $18 pack of four hangover pills.

Not drinking never once occurred to me as a solution for my hangovers. I wasn't an alcoholic so why would I ever stop drinking? I just needed to work to get the hangovers under control. Celery juice helped, overpriced smoothies from smoothie shops sometimes healed, turmeric was a win (inflammation is the cause for everything, amiright?). So many experts gave great advice on what to drink to maintain a healthy figure, how to stay hydrated, and how to bounce back for my morning workout after a night of drinking. There were articles, segments, research and lots of information on how to deal with hangovers and still have a healthy life.

Nothing I read ever indicated that hangovers were optional. They were just what happens when someone consumes too much alcohol; and who hasn't consumed too much alcohol? No websites or health and wellness articles led me to believe that alcohol was related to anxiety. Or

Introduction

that was why, no matter how many interventions I put in place, I couldn't get it under control.

No one told me alcohol causes cancer and many studies show that no amount is safe. No one suggested that I look at my alcohol consumption in the same way wellness experts research carbs and gluten. Not that I remember at least.

I believed that you either drank moderately or you were an alcoholic. As far as I was concerned those categories made up the two (and only two) groups of people in this world. Luckily for me, I was in the group that drank moderately. I could still get hangovers and deal with them by purchasing expensive and organic concoctions from Whole Foods referred to me by fitness kings and queens—people who "knew" health.

Despite my best effort, I couldn't be in both perfect peak health AND drink too much. The hangxiety, headaches, regret, self-loathing, and overall unhappiness wouldn't go away by popping a couple of "hangover pills." I had a decision to make. Ditch booze or continue down this path of blaming my life circumstances on everything but the alcohol?

1

Oh, Not Again!

I woke up with a splitting headache. I had no idea what time it was. The campfire smell in my hair was so strong that I still think of *this* moment every time I smell wood burning. The pull-out couch took up the entire space and it was squeaky when I moved. I was wearing my glasses, which indicated that I had been wise enough to take out my contacts, but I hadn't changed out of my swimsuit. I could tell by the taste in my mouth that I had thrown up. I started to vaguely remember where and when. I slowly turned over to see my sweet four-year-old son lying next to me sound asleep.

Despite the cool temperature in the room, my entire body started sweating profusely. I tried to will myself to remember what happened but I just couldn't put the pieces together. Slowly I pulled myself up and when I stood, I knew I was still pretty drunk. There was so little room around the pull-out couch in the little cabin that I had to crawl over the bed to get to the bathroom. I stood in the bathroom and hovered over the toilet shaking. I prayed that I could throw up again to try to get the poison out of my system. It wasn't happening, and I knew from experience that I would be suffering all day.

I crawled into bed with my husband wondering why I wasn't there in the first place

"Drew, wake up!" I whispered in a hoarse voice.

"Is everything ok?" I asked.

"Yeah. It's fine" he grumbled as he rolled over and made room for me.

He was never as reassuring as I wanted. I desperately wanted him to go over every single detail of the night and tell me that I wasn't the most drunk, that I wasn't too obnoxious and that I didn't make a fool of myself. In other words, I wanted him to lie to me. I already knew exactly what had happened even though I couldn't remember the details.

I had so many questions and I tried to piece together those last few hours. What did I say? Did anyone see me throw up? Was everyone else drunk too? Is anyone else going to feel this hungover? I felt like an awful host, mother and overall human. I wavered between total humiliation and defensiveness. I tried to convince myself that if parenting wasn't so hard, I wouldn't get this way.

I laid there in agony for what felt like years unable to fall back asleep. I berated myself and shamed my behaviors. I welcomed my massive headache and overwhelming nausea as a consequence. Why did I always have to get like this? Why couldn't I keep it under control like everyone else? Why did I perpetually push it to the extreme? My anxiety had been getting worse. I was struggling to decipher between reality and my imagination. Since I couldn't exactly remember, I envisioned terrible things I did and said. I went over every catastrophe that could have happened to my children. I thought of them accidentally wandering into the street or tripping into the fire while I continued sipping from my bottle slurring for them to "watch out" or "stop that."

As the sun finally started to rise and the kids woke, I tried to sense if they knew. Had they seen me slurring my speech and stumbling around? Were they awake when I was throwing up? Did they think something was wrong with me or that I was sick? Luckily, they were oblivious but I still felt a sadness wash over me. I had been lying in bed making promises to myself to be a perfect mother and to never fail them again. They were just babies after all. I had to pull it together. But the second they woke up, I realized I had no strength to be a parent and snapped at them before I even got out of bed.

"Mommy, can I have a snack?" my son asked as I laid in bed unable to move. He was four years old, barely out of diapers. My daughter was only two, sleeping in the pack n play that was set up at the end of the bed.

"We haven't had breakfast yet." I said hoping that he would go crawl back into bed and lay there until I was ready to get up. Something that had never once happened in his lifetime.

"Can I have a snack mommy?" he said in his sweet voice that now felt like nails down a chalkboard.

"No!" I snapped. "We haven't had breakfast. I just told you that." I said sharply, feeling an ache rise in the back of my throat.

Over the past few years I had developed a punishment for my drinking that was both torture and relief. I would attempt to erase the night before with a series of responsible and adult-like actions. I would pretend that everything was fine and make no mention of feeling bad. I would make every effort to appear great, fine, okay...perfect?

I began tidying the tiny cabin. It was the size of a large

bedroom. There was a pull-out couch, two barstools, a tiny kitchen and bathroom and a bedroom with a sink. A few hundred feet away, there was a bunkhouse with only beds. In between was a fire pit area and what we called "The Pavilion" which was just a porch with a picnic table. Mostly used for drinking and mingling with friends that we would bring along with us for long weekends. Like this weekend.

I tried to physically wipe away any evidence that last night had occurred. I gagged down my coffee needing some kind of chemical to counteract the alcohol and I mustered up enough self-hatred to do a few planks and push-ups. I made pancakes from scratch for the kids and even put a little whip cream on them for extra pleasure.

As I wiped, cleaned and finished cooking breakfast, I went over in my head what I would say to my guests who were still sleeping in the bunkhouse. I would most definitely apologize, explaining I didn't know what happened and that I must have gotten too much sun. I would tell them that I was dehydrated. I knew that these were lame excuses and I tried to oppress the memory of the last time I blamed the sun for being blacked out.

Bottom line—I drank too much. The day before, I had cracked open my first 7.5% ABV IPA, then I drank them all day long while we were out on our new boat. We were hosting our good friends and their two children at the lake for the weekend. Then I continued drinking until I could no longer form sentences, thoughts and my body took control by shutting down my brain and expelling the poison.

When everyone else woke up I began the apologies.

"Hey." I said sheepishly to our guests. "I'm so embarrassed. I don't know what happened to me last night. You must think I'm a terrible host." I explained.

"It's fine!" my friend said. "But I knew you were pretty drunk because you just kept repeating the same thing over and over."

The sun shined, the kids played, we ate breakfast and I held back tears as everyone giggled and told me a few "cute" things that I said. Even though nothing bad happened, I felt a familiar sense of remorse and regret. I was both relieved and enraged that no one held me responsible for my behaviors. It's not like I was still in my twenties. I was approaching my mid 30s and this type of behavior wasn't socially acceptable. As a mother of two young children, I was supposed to be responsible. The nagging belief that I should know better wouldn't leave me alone. This was the anxiety portion of my hangover negative self-talk followed by days of worry and fear about what I'd done.

They had no idea. How could they? My friends were completely clueless about my condition and Drew just didn't get it. On the outside everything appeared fine and I knew it. I had spent years mastering the art of not looking anxious and hungover. I had worked very hard to overachieve after a night of drinking to ensure that not a single ounce of evidence that I was out of control was left behind. I didn't speak a word of my blackouts. I didn't speak of my debilitating and irrational thoughts. I covered it all up with acts of perfectionism while feeling worse and worse on a daily basis.

I sat and talked with our friends and gave it my all, trying hard to seem like someone who didn't have a massive hangover. Every time I stepped away to do dishes or get someone more coffee I started to cry and I felt like I could throw up any second. It was too late to go back to bed and our guests were expecting another lake day.

We all piled in the car and headed to the lake for

another day on the water. As we drove, I pressed my cheek against the cool glass of the passenger window. The kids were buckled safely in their car seats and I had packed their water bottles, applied their sunscreen and made sure that we had healthy organic snacks.

I thought back over the last few months and wondered if I might have a drinking problem. I shook as I recalled coming home from Colorado just a month prior in the same physical and mental shape. My friend and I got together for a weekend of dancing and drinking and I couldn't remember any of our time together. I had blamed that on the altitude and the gin, but no one else seemed to be in my condition. I began to badger the guitarist at the bar by begging him to play Counting Crows songs and "Sweet Child O' Mine" by Guns N' Roses. When he ignored me and continued to play whatever he was playing I told him he sucked. I don't remember exactly but I can envision myself swaying and slurring while feeling irritated. Shortly after that, we were asked to leave. On the plane ride home, I swore that I would never drink again. For a few days, I didn't.

Then my mind slipped back just a little further to when we celebrated my parents 50th wedding anniversary. I decided to stay up and wait for the arrival of my cousins while pounding beers late into the night. Again I woke up in a daze, this time next to my two-year-old baby girl promising God that I would never "get like this" again. But that same night, when my sister and I hosted my parents' surprise party, I proudly held up my glass for a toast and started the cycle over again.

As we pulled into the marina on this beautiful Sunday morning, I remember the sky was big and blue. Everyone was happy and relaxed. Families were smiling as they loaded their floats, coolers and towels out of their cars and onto their boats. The marina picnic tables were full of people already having ice cream and jalapeño poppers while wearing their lifejackets. Nearby, a boat was pulled up blaring Kenny Chesney's "Summertime," a song that I would normally love, but at the moment I wanted it to go away.

It was a picture-perfect day. One that I would long for all winter, but I was barely hanging on. I shut my eyes tight and they burned from exhaustion and dehydration. I silently prayed for a thunderstorm or severe lightning so that I would have an excuse to go back home, crawl into bed, and close the curtains. I felt terrified that the boat would wreck or that there would be too much weight in the coolers and it would capsize. I had a feeling that something terrible was going to happen any second. I knew that this was just my version of a hangover but I couldn't stop shaking and my heart was pounding out of my chest.

Riding out on the boat to our swimming spot I covered myself with a towel. When the boat stopped, I forced a smile on my face and apologized for not being "very talkative" as the rest of the group cracked open a fresh beer. I knew that there was no way I could drink and I was relieved. Normally more beer would be the perfect cure for my anxiety but I just couldn't. Maybe it was exhaustion. Maybe I was too physically shaky to reach into the cooler. Maybe just maybe I'd finally had enough.

2

Growing Up Anxious

I grew up in the 80s and 90s in a very small town in rural Kentucky. It was right off a major highway and there was a long strip of fast food restaurants and gas stations making it appear like it might be an actual city. But once you passed the Dairy Queen it became pretty desolate, with fewer and fewer stores and buildings. There was a K-Mart and a local grocery store named Ralph's, after the owner. There was a drug store which also served as a gift shop. There were three schools—elementary, middle and high. Everyone knew each other by their first names and if you ever happened to run into someone you didn't know, the person you were with would clear it right up by saying something like "Oh, that's Jim's oldest daughter."

Growing up in a small town is so different from living in a city. Knowing people everywhere you go inspires a strong sense of community. On Friday nights, you could find the whole town at the high school football or basketball games. We had parades down Main Street for holidays like Christmas and Memorial Day and everyone you knew would be there watching the homemade floats go by. If you forgot your wallet when you went to the grocery store, you could leave with your groceries and pay later. If you wanted clothes from the town's one clothing store, you could pick some out, take them home to try on and bring back whatever you didn't want, paying for what you kept. If your car broke down, someone would stop to help you right away.

There wasn't much to do, so people had to come up with their own fun. Cruising was a thing. You could find twenty or more cars parked in the hardware store parking lot on summer nights. People would drive a loop around the McDonald's, down to a stop light, then back to a parking lot. There, you would sit in your car, talk, listen to music and when you got bored you would cruise that same loop again. And again. In high school, if I wanted to find someone I knew, I would head straight for the hardware store (Farmer's) and look there first.

There was a general sense of easy living. Limited stores and restaurants meant fewer decisions. If you wanted a pizza, you got one from Pizza Hut. If you wanted ice cream, you would go to Dairy Queen. If you wanted coffee, you would make it at home. If you wanted alcohol, well, that's a different story. My small town was in a "dry" county. "Dry" means that you can't buy or sell alcohol anywhere within the county limits. So if you wanted alcohol, you could either drive to the next town over, which was about 30 minutes away, or you could run up to the bootlegger. A bootlegger is defined as someone who manufactures or sells alcohol illegally, but we just thought of him as a nice guy who was saving us a trip.

When it came to alcohol and drinking, it seemed to me that there were three camps of people living in my small town. There were those who believed that if you drank you were damned to hell. These were the people who considered drinking the biggest of all sins (right up there with being gay and of course using the Lord's name in vain). Then, there were those who believed that drinking could make for a good time. These were people who seemed to also love God and went to church every Sunday. They just thought there was nothing wrong with a stiff drink right after work or a few drinks around the pool on a hot Saturday night. Finally, there were those who abused alcohol and became drunks. These people definitely didn't go to church and could be found stumbling around town holding onto something in a brown paper bag. Everybody knew a drunk. A cousin that no longer came around, an uncle that sometimes started an argument or a neighbor that you could overhear yelling in their house after a few too many.

My parents were in the camp that believed drinking made for a good time. My dad grew up on a farm in rural Kentucky that really hasn't changed much at all in 80 years. He walked to school barefoot (literally) and his family made money by selling eggs and meat from the animals they raised on the land. He met a buddy that lived down the street. They had heard of construction work paying big bucks in Chicago and as soon as they graduated from high school, they went. It wasn't long before they met sisters.

My mom was an Italian Catholic living on the outskirts of the city. Her parents owned a gas station and market that her mother mostly ran by herself. Her father drove a city bus. My mom had two brothers and a sister and they all lived nearby. Her family started to marry and have kids all around the same time, so my parents began their first married years in the suburbs of Chicago. My sister was born there and my parents love to tell stories about the big family gatherings they had. Easter parades, Christmas parties, New Year's Eve dances and something to celebrate almost every weekend. It was a very different life that I only knew about from the stories and pictures.

Once I was born my parents moved to the country to be closer to my dad's family and the farm. They left behind my mom's big family and all of their friends. They also left behind the city lights and all the cannolis, wine and lasagnas that my mom was so used to having around. It must have been a shock for her to move somewhere where you couldn't even buy alcohol.

My mom had a northern accent and said things like "Ma" (the name of her mother) and "pop" for the kind of soda that she was drinking. My dad had a twang in his talk and called the place where he grew up a "holler" while he slurped up his milk and cornbread. There was a drastic difference in their upbringing and also their personalities. My mom was social and enjoyed being around people, going places and having fun. My dad was a loner, quiet and loved nothing more than staying home. Regardless of their differences, they were happily married.

I wasn't surrounded by alcohol all the time. My dad drank Budweiser usually, but on Christmas and other holidays he would sip apricot brandy that my cousins would bring back from Chicago. My mom would drink one sweet drink like a mudslide once a month or so. Seeing a beer bottle on the table or a Budweiser in the fridge was the same to me as seeing a loaf of bread or a carton of eggs. It was just…there.

As a child I can remember seeing advertisements for alcohol. There were beer commercials with beautiful people at the beach or at a party having the time of their lives. There were the ones about men in suits drinking something brown out of a fancy glass with a big giant ice cube. There were the strong horses and the snow-covered mountains. The ads mostly seemed targeted toward men but women were always around smiling and looking happy. The commercials showed that drinking was life enhancing, fun and desirable.

I saw the same theme play out in movies. I loved to watch the movie *Dirty Dancing*. I was mostly drawn to the music and the dance scenes. But I remember perfectly one of the opening scenes where Baby finds her way to the staff party and everyone is drinking, dancing and having fun. I remember thinking that I couldn't wait to get older. I wanted to wear crop tops, dance the night away and hold an amber bottle in my hand.

I also picked up on the idea that drinking too much could make you drunk. It was clear, even as a child, that's exactly what happened to poor Mrs. Hannigan in *Annie* (another childhood favorite). She was stumbling, mumbling and always appeared angry. She was clearly in the camp of "drunk," and even back then, I figured there must be something wrong with her.

Based on the movies I watched, commercials I saw and the casual drinking of my own parents, I began to form some beliefs related to alcohol. I assumed that there were two types of drinkers in the world; drinkers (like Baby's friends) and drunks (like Mrs. Hannigan). I believed drinkers to be beautiful, cool, fun, eccentric and alive. They listened to great music, they danced, they traveled, they ate yummy meals that paired perfectly with their drink. They were carefree and happy. They laughed a lot and smiled endlessly. They held fancy glasses, had a spread of garnishes like cherries or orange slices, or a cellar full of wine. They were smart, sophisticated, but also daring and exciting. They were sometimes outdoorsy as they sipped their concoctions outside by a fire wearing sweaters.

I believed the drunks were sweaty and jobless. They

could be found in dark, scary bars during the day. They wobbled around and slurred their speech. They caused trouble and started fights. They were loud, obnoxious and sometimes abusive. They were careless, forgetful, and put their children in unsafe situations. They needed some kind of help.

I don't remember anyone explaining to me the difference between drunks and regular drinkers. These ideas just kind of formed. My parents certainly didn't talk about drinking in this way. They didn't talk about it much at all actually. Alcohol only showed up as safe and fun in my life. I had the luxury of never being around an abusive drunk and my parents sheltered me from seeing any inappropriate alcohol-induced situations.

In elementary school, a DARE (Drug Abuse Resistance Education) officer came to my school. He showed the students pictures of cars piled on top of one another on a highway with mangled parts and broken glass everywhere. He explained that car wrecks are what happen when you drink and drive. It scared me. I got the message loud and clear that I should never drink and drive. But I don't remember the DARE officer saying, "don't drink."

I hadn't seen people doing drugs. No adults that I knew did those. That seemed scary and dangerous and I was grossed out when the DARE officer showed images of drug users. My parents even talked about how bad drugs were for you. Drugs are dangerous. Drugs can kill you. Drugs will ruin your life. The words, the images and the messages were seared into my brain. Say no to drugs.

Our home was in a small neighborhood. We had brownish orange carpeting and a built-in couch covered in the same color. The walls were paneled and there was brown trim. I had the middle bedroom. For my 10th birthday I got to redo the whole room in a Mickey Mouse theme. Yes, at the age of 10 I was still very much into Mickey Mouse.

We painted the walls white, got a black and white ceiling fan, decorated with my Disney toys and I had a Mickey blanket.

My sister had the bedroom at the end of the hall until she went away to college. I was only six years old. She's twelve years older than me and we didn't have much in common. When she had friends over, I would wait outside her bedroom trying to hear their conversations. I so desperately wanted her to let me into her room. I would bang on the door or wiggle my fingers in the tiny opening under the door, hoping that she would one day graciously invite me in. But she was way too cool for that. She did things like drive, go to prom and hang out with boys. I thought that she was living the life of a movie star. Her big hair, jean jacket and blue eye shadow made me swoon and I tried everything to mimic her look. I would sneak into her room and steal her makeup, I borrowed her scarves and old t-shirts and I would tease my hair to get it as big as possible. Looking back at pictures, I'm in shock at the clothes that I would consider outfits. I would wear a swimsuit (in the winter) under washed out jean shorts, with neon colored socks and a big giant bow. Sometimes if I was lucky, my sister would play her Go Go's record for me and tell me about music she liked. I loved everything about her. She seemed more like a rad roommate than a sister.

"Are you wearing that out?" I asked her one day as she was sitting on the floor in her room getting ready in front of the mirror wearing her bra.

"Yea." she said as she stroked on mascara and teased her red hair.

"I'm telling Dad." I threatened.

"Go ahead." she said applying lipstick and spraying enough Aqua Net to kill a small animal.

I didn't go and tell my dad because I was too mesmerized by her makeup application. I sat at the door to her room watching the whole thing feeling both jealous and excited.

Once my sister moved out, I always felt a little nervous. The quiet house felt deafening. I didn't understand my anxious feelings, but once she moved out I ached for another child around, a playmate or a friend. Maybe something to distract me from "that feeling." The one where my hands would sweat and my heart would beat fast. The one that made me feel like it was hard to breathe sometimes. The one that made me feel like something was wrong.

It was just me and my parents. It was quiet and I didn't like it. My dad liked to sit at the tiny, round kitchen table playing solitaire. My mom sometimes worked at K-Mart in the evenings, leaving me to play with my cabbage patch dolls or watch TV. My sister would come back and visit a lot. She was there for every holiday and family gathering and I loved it when we were all back together as a family. I wanted her to stay longer and live there with us again but I don't think I ever uttered these words to anyone.

I was a social kid. I liked playing with friends and being around people. My quiet home didn't mesh well with my outgoing, lively personality and I was always yearning for more action and more fun. Being social was kind of like a coping skill. It was a distraction. An escape of sorts. When I was alone with my thoughts, I would sometimes think up bad things. Like an intruder coming into the house while we were sleeping or getting lost from my parents in the grocery store. It was scary how real it felt. I was terrified of the dark and begged my mom to sleep with me on a regular basis. When I was nervous I could feel my heart beating out of my chest and my palms would get so sweaty that it would drip down my wrists. I kept this all a secret. Afraid that if I said it out loud it would grow.

When I was still in elementary school my parents opened a balloon shop. Yep. We sold balloons to make a living. It wasn't just balloons. It was more a novelty shop plus balloons, like a hospital gift shop but on the corner of Main Street for everyone to see. The shop had a glass door and a bell rang when someone would open it.

In the front of the shop were shelves displaying stuffed animals, small toys, baskets and candy. The walls were lined with mylar balloons for display so that the customer could just point to the one that they wanted. Toward the back there was a giant popcorn maker like the kind you see at a baseball game, a cash register, a desk and a door to the back room.

That was my room. I didn't sleep there but there was a bed, some shelves, big boxes filled with goods and stuff for the shop, and around the corner was a toilet. I grew up in the back of the "shop" which had my own little toys and a basket for me to use to get popcorn from the popcorn machine any time I wanted. To this day, popcorn is my favorite snack.

If I was thirsty, I would walk up the street to the hardware store where the owners sold Coca Cola out of their green and white Coleman cooler for 50 cents each. When I got bored I would head over to the town salon, and beg the owner to let me use the products and brushes as I watched her cut, perm, and style the customers' hair. I would swing myself round and round and up and down in the salon chair until she would kindly send me on my way. Then, I would run down to the dress shop and hang out with my friend from school. We would stand in the windows with the mannequins and play in the dressing rooms when there was no one shopping.

The balloon shop closed at 5 pm, so I would always arrive back at the shop just as my parents were locking the door. We would head home, just the three of us, while I longed for more distraction. That "feeling" would come back. Especially as it got closer to nighttime. It came on slowly. I would feel a ping of dread followed by worry. I was afraid of the dark. I believed there were monsters in my closet and I slept with my arms tucked under the blanket because I thought if I let them dangle from the bed something scary would grab my hand. Fast heartbeat, sweaty hands, shortness of breath and worry. I would worry about my parents dying or I would worry my friends were mad at me, or if I said something embarrassing. If there was nothing tangible to worry about, I made up things. What if the house catches on fire? What if I can't find my backpack in the morning? My worry ranged from big to small things, but they were equally as disturbing to me. I didn't have any reason for this worry. My parents weren't sick and I didn't know anyone's parents who were. My friends were generally nice to me. I wasn't too awkward or too ugly and I knew how to fit in. Regardless, the worry was endless. Sometimes I had trouble making it stop.

When a storm would come or the wind blew, my whole body would tense and feel shaky. I was sure it meant a tornado was coming and the wind would blow the roof off our house. I would ask my parents questions about the weather and make up a safety plan of getting in the bathtub if I heard the storm sirens. There was no convincing myself it was just a little rain. I always thought the worst was coming.

I would try to distract myself with activity and noise. I

would ask to invite friends over and we would stay awake as late as we could so I wouldn't have to face the worry. I would listen to music loudly. As I got older I would watch hours and hours of *The Real World* on MTV. While I was engaged in someone else's world I didn't have to worry about mine. It was good to get away from my thoughts for awhile. I was always looking for ways to escape the fear.

One night, in the fall of my freshman year of high school I woke up gasping for air. I couldn't breathe. I sat up and yanked off the covers, trying to figure out what was happening and finally caught my breath. I woke up my parents and told them what happened. I described it to them as choking.

For the next few months I refused to go to sleep. I was terrified that I would stop breathing. I told my parents (and myself) that when I laid down it "started to happen." My throat would close up and I would have trouble breathing. So instead of going to bed I would stay up as late as I could watching C-SPAN with my dad only allowing my eyes to close when I could no longer control being awake.

During this time my parents were very worried and supportive. Since I had described to them the feeling that I was choking, we visited my doctor to figure out what was wrong with my throat.

"Tell me what happened Samantha," a female doctor asked as I sat on the cold exam table with the crackly white paper.

"When I lay down, it feels like my throat is starting to close and I begin to choke" I explained as my heart pounded and armpits dripped with sweat.

"Does your stomach ever hurt?" she asked.

"Yes, sometimes" I replied wondering why she was talking to me about my stomach when the problem was in my throat.

"I think I know what the problem is." she said as a wave of relief came over my body and I thought I might jump up to hug her.

After a series of tests, scans and blood work she diagnosed me with acid reflux. This was before mental health awareness was a thing. Not a word was mentioned about anxiety. No one once gave me the side-eye or suggested that maybe what I felt was a panic attack. No one asked me if I had nervous thoughts or went over any symptoms of anxiety. I don't think I had ever really even heard the word "anxiety" before. My description was accurate and my symptoms were authentic. It never even occurred to me that I might be choking because of irrational fear.

Before I knew it, my parents propped my bed up on wooden slats in order to prevent the acid from building up while I was lying flat. I was prescribed antacids. The diagnosis appeased me and, most importantly, I had a plan. If I felt like I couldn't breathe, I could take the antacids and get out of bed. I could sleep again instantly and everyone was relieved. But there was always this fear that lingered in the back of my mind. The question, "What if I stop breathing again?" was always there.

The fear followed me right into college and throughout my adult life. It wasn't always about breathing. Sometimes it was just a feeling of nervousness, a sense of doom, a question of safety or a lingering uneasy feeling.

3

My First Hangovers

During high school, I had volunteered with our Special Olympics program. Despite my not-perfect GPA and crappy test-taking skills, I caught the attention of a group of people who awarded college scholarships to students who worked and contributed to society through volunteering. I did very well in the interview process and won the scholarship.

This scholarship was amazing, but I was too immature and naive to really understand how much college cost. My high school was easy. I made pretty good grades, but I wouldn't say that I necessarily applied myself. I studied just enough to get by, borrowed notes from friends and took easy classes. I didn't challenge myself in any way. I was focused on the social aspects of high school, which I continued right into my freshman year of college.

As soon as I arrived on campus in the fall of 1999, I felt a daring sense of freedom. I couldn't believe that I was allowed to do whatever I wanted without anyone checking in. There were no real rules, no curfews, no one to report to, no supervision whatsoever! Most importantly, there were lots and lots of people. In the hallways, on the campus and even in the city of Lexington. There were more people than I had ever been around before. I was so excited!

One night, after shortly arriving on campus, a friend I knew from my hometown invited me to her apartment for a party. She was a good friend from high school, but two years older than me. She asked me what I wanted to drink because I needed somebody older to buy my alcohol. I decided on a bottle of Arbor Mist. I must have overheard someone else getting this, because I'd never had it before. It was wine, I guess. Wine with added sugar and sweeteners. I remember that I chose peach flavor because I loved peach flavored Snapple tea and I assumed peach wine would taste the same.

I drank the whole bottle through a straw—the giant kind you get with a Big Gulp. The apartment was filled with strangers. A few people my age, a few older, but everyone seemed so grown up to me. We hung out while dancing, having deep conversations (as deep as an 18-year-old drinking wine through a straw could have) and listening to *really* good music. The kind that I hadn't listened to much in my hometown. Dave Matthews Band and Widespread Panic weaved their way into my body and I couldn't tell if I was drunk or if it was just the bliss of my new life unfolding ahead of me.

I woke up on the couch in the middle of the night because my body was shaking. I was wearing bib overalls with a maroon spaghetti strap tank top. I thought this outfit was sexy because you could see my bare waist a bit where the shirt ended before the jeans started. At that moment, however, my clothes felt itchy and heavy. I crawled to my friend's bedroom and woke her up.

"Wake up. I need help." I said as I laid on the floor next to her bed, unable to stand up.

"I'm going to be sick." I told her.

"Go to the bathroom," she said. Then she fell back asleep.

I slept next to the toilet the rest of the night. The room was spinning and I needed water badly, but there was no way I could move. I finally puked and felt a little better. The whole next day was ruined. I was tired, shaky and so nauseous. I hated feeling that terrible and wondered why my friends didn't seem to be in the same awful condition. I wallowed, agonized and felt humiliated every time I thought of myself stumbling around with my wine bottle and giant straw. It felt dramatic, like maybe the worst thing that ever happened. I took pain relievers, cried and slept on and off. It felt like the worst case of the flu. I wondered if I could be dying. No one else seemed to feel as bad as I did. No one else was crying and wallowing. I blamed the straw. I somehow lived through the day, but decided never to drink again. Never drink peach wine that is.

Moving to Lexington and attending the University of Kentucky was a big change considering the small town I'd come from. I lived in a co-ed dorm. To me, it felt like it had 100 floors with alternating floors being girls and guys. I quickly made friends with other girls on the fourth floor and they knew a group of guys that lived a few floors up. When I wasn't invited to any parties, we hung out in our dorm rooms listening to music and drinking massive amounts of whatever shitty beer someone's friend who was 21 would buy for us. Technically, our campus was "dry" meaning we weren't allowed to have alcohol in our rooms.

One night, we were listening to music in our dorm while drinking and talking. The room was a very narrow

200 square-foot space. It had two tiny twin beds, a little walkway down the middle, and a desk at the end of each bed. Above the bed, was a shelf where I kept the snacks my parents would send me and I had a microwave and a mini fridge. There was a closet and even a small space with a mirror for getting ready. Despite the cramped space, we managed to fit a pretty big group of about 12 people in my room. For someone who had never really gone to parties in high school, this seemed like a good start and I was happy.

As the night went on the music got louder and the drinks made me bolder. There was a knock at the door and I eagerly answered it holding a beer can in my hand. It was my floors' Resident Assistant.

"Is there drinking going on here?" she asked awkwardly, already knowing the answer.

I stared at her, unable to speak, but flashed a big ignorant smile.

"Everyone out!" she said, holding open the door and ushering folks back to their rooms.

The next morning there was a pink slip under my door. It was a citation for underage drinking and violating the dry campus rule. My punishment was a $65 fine and a mandatory class called Choices. It felt like a really big deal and $65 was a lot of money to me at the time. I couldn't ask my parents for it and I didn't yet have a job, so I had to borrow some of the money from a friend. Choices was supposed to be a learning tool that would scare me into no longer drinking...on campus. But many of my friends received the same citation, so we piled in our cars and attended the class on the same Saturday. We ate lunch together during our break and afterward went out drinking to celebrate a hard day's work.

While the social aspects of college were easy for me,

the academic parts were a challenge. I didn't realize the demands in college were so much higher. I actually needed to go to class and then study the materials given in order to be an average student—at the very least. But I didn't. I rarely made it to class and when I did, I was so behind that it was pointless because there was no catching up. By the end of the first semester I had lost my full ride scholarship. I was failing most of my classes and not keeping the GPA requirement. I tried to come up with a million excuses. I wrote letters to the Board of the scholarship, begging for a second chance. I explained that I had been sick a lot and provided them with doctor's notes. It was kind of true. I had pink eye that lasted for more than two weeks. I pleaded that I was just a child and had no idea how to cope with college in a big city having come from such a small town. I promised that if I could have another chance, I would take college seriously and make good grades. But they declined, as they should have, and I faced the biggest of all consequences for my poor choices. I devastated my parents. I disappointed everyone in my small town who knew I threw away my amazing opportunity. And, I never forgave myself for winning the scholarship over applicants who would have done a better job, who could have stayed the path, wouldn't have partied their way through their first semester. I was ashamed.

Alcohol and college were best friends. Everyone drank. Parties, socials, study clubs and bars were always happening and bursting with students. Bud Light became my drink of choice. I loved the way the thin, amber bottle felt in my hand. I would peel away at the label at every football game, sorority social that I was invited to, and parties that I was too young to attend. The bottle became my friend, my confidant, my escape from anxious feelings when I was in a social setting. It gave me something to do with all of that awkward and nervous energy. I felt cool. Like I fit in, even though my outfits weren't that great, my hair wasn't blonde and I wasn't a member of the sorority or club.

I was a fun drunk. I was always the first on the dance floor, the one singing karaoke, the girl dragging her friends to hear the next band. It was mostly innocent with very few, if any, ramifications. Everyone was doing it and nothing seemed out of the ordinary at all. We drank most weekends and slept all day Sunday while rehashing all the funny things that happened.

It didn't occur to me that in between drinking and partying, some of my friends hit the library to study every once in a while. Many of them had learned study skills in high school and knew what it took to make good grades. Many of them did, in fact, make it to their 8 am Spanish class even though we said "screw it" the night before. But I assumed that we were all just hanging around having the time of our lives.

Was it the time of our lives? I started noticing that my throat felt like it was closing again. I had learned by now that it was called anxiety. I would have scary thoughts and worry about things that would probably never happen. I made up stories like what if someone kidnapped me as I walked across campus or someone brought a gun to one of my classes. I hated being alone because the thoughts would grow. I also felt very depressed and lonely after the party was over. While everyone was relaxed and laughing off the night before, I was always left feeling edgy.

As I got closer to my senior year, I decided to take advantage of the campus health benefits. I made an appointment to see a doctor. I told him that I thought I might have anxiety. I'd heard this word a few times by now, both in my classes and from meeting a few people who experienced anxiety. I wanted help. I described my worried thoughts, racing heart, sweaty palms and the general sense of nervousness I had been experiencing since childhood. The doctor diagnosed me with general anxiety disorder and prescribed Lexapro.

At first, I was so relieved. That feeling had a name and actual diagnosis that could be treated. It was anxiety. I would take medication and all the worry would go away and I would never have to feel that way again. But it wasn't quite as easy as I hoped. Suddenly, my edge was gone. I felt completely lethargic. I couldn't wake up in the mornings and I felt tired all the time. I didn't feel fun either. I felt "meh" which was better than feeling anxious but still not great. It didn't occur to me to wonder if I should be drinking while taking the medication. If maybe the two were a bad combo and causing some of the side effects. Not drinking would not have been an option.

I began to wonder if my anxiety was actually a good thing. The thing that motivated me, gave me drive and kept me alert. I stopped taking the Lexapro and never went back to the doctor. I never felt anxious when I was drinking anyway, so I figured I could just use alcohol to relax.

By the time I turned 21, I befriended a guy in a band. This meant I spent my time hanging out in every bar they played, drinking before the show, during the show and for the after party. I was a "Band Aid" as I liked to call myself and took that role as seriously as someone getting a Harvard Law degree. I would show up hours before the band went on, while they were setting up, and would start drinking. Then, I would stay after the show and wait while they took down their equipment and slowly loaded their cars. Sometimes I took my last sip of alcohol while stumbling out of the closing bar at 4 am.

One night I was so drunk that I was stumbling all over the place, knocking over drinks and falling into people. The bouncers kicked me out of the bar, so I sat outside on the bench between the entrance and the small alley parking lot. I was swaying back and forth and if I could have formed sentences, I would have asked someone to go find my friends.

I squinted through the window and could make out a blurred vision of the bouncers standing there pointing and laughing at something. I was too confused to see what it was but a little crowd had seemed to gather as I sat there swaying and trying to mumble that I just "needed a minute." Finally, I could no longer hold back and I puked all down the front of my clothes and all over the sidewalk leading into the bar. The bouncers looked angry and seemed to be yelling something at me as I laid all the way down on the bench and closed my eyes.

Hours later, the band finished their set and scooped me up for the afterparty. When we arrived at the bass player's girlfriend's apartment, I changed into some of her clothes and washed mine out in her bathroom sink. It occurred to me that I was surrounded by mostly strangers and I felt alone and sad. "What is happening to my life?" I thought.

As the weekends with the band would come to an end and everyone pulled themselves back together, I was left with a loneliness and sadness that I couldn't describe. I had this underlying demon that would build up, making me feel like there was always something wrong, something scary. In fact, sometimes this edge was so bad that I found myself looking for someone to go out with on Sunday nights. I didn't want to be alone. Even though the thought of drinking made me sick, I couldn't think of anything else to do. So I would find someone, anyone, to meet me at a bar.

By some miracle, I was able to graduate from college. It took a while (five years) and I changed majors from special education to psychology. I loved my psychology classes. I took a class on death and dying that taught me so much about how we view death in our culture. I took a women's history class that blew my mind. I loved my social behaviors class, which taught me about human tendencies. I was even able to land a few very cool internships working with children with Autism.

My internships, psychology degree and work experience helped me find a job in social work right out of college. It was in Louisville, about an hour from where I lived in Lexington and even further from my parents. I knew a lot of people living there, including some of my old college roommates, so I was happy to move. I worked for a community mental health agency. I immediately fell in love with social work and worked around some supportive and passionate people.

The "center" as we called it was always bustling. People would come there to receive help for their mental health needs. My specific job was to work with children who had emotional and behavioral disorders. I wouldn't say I was prepared for that type of work, but the job was my calling. I was barely an adult myself and I loved working with high schoolers and children.

Somehow, I instinctively knew just what to do. I wasn't at all shaken by stories of abuse and neglect. I wasn't uncomfortable with sadness or depression. I didn't flinch when someone shared their disturbing thoughts or feelings. Instead I was filled with compassion, empathy and a deep-rooted desire to help.

This was also my first experience with mentorship. In

college my class sizes were very large. I often wondered if there was a single teacher who even knew what I looked like. I'd heard stories of people having deep relationships with professors who had taken them under their wings and shown them the ropes. I could barely even remember what building my classes were in, let alone form relationships. At my new job, my boss took an interest in my work. She led through discussion and experience. She allowed me to try new things and make mistakes. When I failed we came up with a better plan together. I felt completely comfortable telling her when there was a therapeutic technique that I didn't understand or I felt like I had no idea what I was doing.

"Okay, hang on," she would say, as she gathered a few books and materials for me to go over so I could learn more on the topic.

This type of hands-on experience was my learning style. I liked it far better than anything I'd ever done in college. I loved shadowing, watching and seeing the work of others. I started reading as many books as possible and taking notes. I went to every single training available. I asked to sit in with other, more experienced therapists and professionals. I volunteered to do anything that needed to be done so that I could gain experience. I was eager. I was surprised at how much I loved learning, especially when I was seen and supported. The sadness hit me again regarding the loss of my college scholarship. The regret was deep.

I was also learning in other ways. I was meeting people who came from different places with different backgrounds. Each time I sat with a new family listening to their life stories, my experience with the world shifted. I was no longer in a bubble where everyone was exactly like me. I learned that some people were born into a world of chaos and danger. They had already experienced trauma that they would spend their whole lives trying to unravel. These interactions made me realize that there weren't bad people in the world. Instead, bad things happen to people. I learned that the systems were broken and the cycles repeated. I learned to have empathy for hardship and fear I hadn't personally experienced. I learned the absolute importance of an individual's basic needs being met. And I found out what happens to the brains of people who live without food, shelter, safety and belonging—and therefore their lives.

Instead of worrying about myself, I was able to listen to people's most vulnerable life events and actually help or add value. When I was working at the center, I rarely felt anxiety because my actual job was to help make safety plans and treatment guides to mitigate a crisis. In the presence of drama I was cool as a cucumber. I discovered it was the absence of drama that fed my anxiety.

I had a focus, a career and the actual chance at making a difference. I was growing up and even though drinking was still a major factor, with my new job, I kept it mostly confined to weekends. Most of my friends still partied. We went all out on Friday and Saturdays. There were always concerts, events and bars. Better yet—now we had enough money to buy tickets, pay cover charges, buy more drinks. I would get really drunk most weekends. On Sundays I would wake up vowing to never drink again.

I hated feeling hungover. I would spend the day rehashing the details of the weekend and worrying about things. I worried about what I said, the people I hung out with, the money I'd spent, my lack of sleep, the weight I was gaining and other things. This is when the Sunday night blues set in. When the party was over and the drinking had stopped, I experienced horrendous anxiety.

This anxiety was now something that I predicted would be a part of my hangovers. My chest would pound most of the day and I would have trouble sleeping. I would lay awake at night fearing the worst. I considered seeing a doctor, but remembered how horrible I felt when I took medication and decided I was better off without it.

Things felt complicated at times. I didn't feel good about myself. I felt like I should be making more money. I should be married. I should be more put together. I should be able to buy clothes from responsible stores like Banana Republic. I should be able to sign up to bring something other than paper cups to the office potluck. Literally, the idea of having it together enough to be able to shop for ingredients and cook something to bring to work the next day was astonishing to me. I didn't have a clue how to be an adult despite getting older by the minute. I was only 24 years old, but I felt like life was passing me by.

One day I was standing in line to get a sandwich at Subway. I didn't have a single dime to my name and had been living on my Discover card to buy everything from gas, beers and apparently now sandwiches. I had gained at least 20 pounds and started feeling pretty depressed and lonely, despite being surrounded by tons of friends most of the time. My high school friends were married or getting married, some friends were starting to buy houses and others were beginning to start a family. It occurred to me that spending my days trying to score concert tickets and buying clothes to go out in were kind of shallow and immature. I wanted a change but wasn't exactly sure what to do about it.

As I got to my turn in line, I got a text from one of my best high school friends.

"We just bought a house!!!!" I read on my phone in disbelief.

"American or Provolone" the guy said from behind the counter as I stared at my phone wondering where on Earth I had gone wrong with everything.

"Ma'am?" the man said loudly.

"Huh, I'm sorry what did you say?" I asked after I realized that I wasn't paying a bit of attention.

"American or Provolone" he repeated to me in a tone that made it clear that I wasn't the only one hating my life at that moment.

"American." I said realizing that this was the biggest decision that I would face on this day.

I handed over my Discover card as my cheeks turned red with shame. I charged four dollars and 35 cents worth of a turkey sandwich, cool ranch Doritos, and a Diet Coke because I didn't have enough money to buy it outright. This was a turning point for me. It's not that I wanted to buy a house right away, but that question flooded back to the surface leaving a burning feeling inside my chest "What am I doing?"

I coped with this news by doing the thing I did best. I found someone/anyone to go out with me and get completely hammered. I used that same, nearly maxed out, credit card to buy everyone drinks. Instead of focusing on the thing that was really bothering me, I subconsciously created other problems to distract me from having to face my life. By this time, I was too far into credit card debt to ask anyone for help. I was ashamed to let anyone know that I couldn't afford a single thing. I distinctly remember that all of sudden every ad on the radio was about how to get out of debt.

"Are you in debt with no way out? We can help. Call today."

Instead of calling, I just pushed the subject as far down as I could and did anything to avoid thinking about it.

Drinking was great at making sure I didn't have to think and so, at the time, it seemed like the only solution. But every time I handed over my card to pay the tab, my heart would pound and my hands would sweat as I wondered if this would be the time it was denied.

4

Meeting My Drinking Buddy

It was a Sunday night and I was having an awful case of the Sunday night blues. After a weekend spent drinking with friends, the party was over and I was alone with my thoughts, exhausted, hungover and broke. At age 26, I was old enough to know better but still very young and immature. My roommate popped into my room and told me that she and her boyfriend were going to get ice cream and asked me if I wanted to come along. The answer was always yes. Anything to not be alone!

I was wearing an old Chicago Cubs tee with ratty gym shorts that I had slept in the night before and my glasses. As we walked to the ice cream place close to our house, my roommate's boyfriend suggested stopping by his friend's house. We approached the front door of a cute Cape Cod literally one block away from our place. We knocked on the door and the soon-to-be love of my life answered.

He was very tall, at least a foot taller than me. I looked past him into his home and found it to be very tidy, well decorated and smelling of citrus and Irish spring soap. I did a quick mental check of my space—a mattress on slats, floor covered in clothes, it basically looked like the room of a teenage girl in comparison to this adult home I was seeing. The guy at the door seemed mature and grown up and I suddenly wished I had put in my contacts and changed out of my pajamas. He had this deep voice that didn't seem to quite match his long, lean stature.

His name was Drew and I wouldn't say I was immediately drawn to him, but there was something different about him that interested me. My dating life had been tough and I sucked at relationships. I was focused on going out and having fun, which came with drama, fighting and bad decisions when it came to guys.

As we walked to the corner creamery I hung back with my roommate and talked to her while not really thinking much about him. When we stood in line to order my mouth was watering as I decided on the peanut butter cup ice cream with a cookie crumble topping. Drew was standing in line in front of me and I heard him place his order

"I'll have one scoop of vanilla frozen yogurt, please." he told the clerk with confidence.

What? I thought. *Why in the hell would he order something so healthy?* My mind was scrambling as I tried to think of the most nutritious choice at the ice cream shop without copying his order. I suddenly didn't want to give off the impression that I only ate garbage.

"I'll have a strawberry smoothie." I said as beads of sweat broke out on my forehead.

I can't remember one word we said to each other that night, but somehow I felt the tides shift. Earlier that year I had made a pact with a friend. We decided that we were no longer going to wait to be selected by guys, instead we would be the ones selecting. Most of my other friends were married or planning their weddings. Some were already having children and more had bought houses. I wanted to get serious about my future and being in a relationship would be a start.

I called myself the *Selector*. Mostly as a joke but also not. I changed my computer passwords at work to "Selector." I doodled the word on notebooks. I would repeat it in my head as I was talking to random guys at bars. On this night, at this place, I had a strong, undeniable urge to select.

I learned that Drew was a banker and a triathlete. He'd had a few serious relationships, but no major baggage. He seemed responsible, kind and exuded a strong sense of financial stability.

I couldn't understand what he liked about me. By this time I was in serious credit card debt from buying going out clothes at Forever 21, putting all the shots on my tab and charging enough Victoria's Secret *Love Spell* body spray to poison a small rodent. The only things I truly owned were the pack of cigarettes in my purse and a quilt knitted by my grandmother. Also, my idea of exercise was standing in line to use the bathroom at bars.

At first, our dates happened at bars. We would hang with our mutual friends for a night of drinking and dancing. We would both get sloppy drunk and end the night sleeping over at each other's houses. Since I had roommates we would mostly stay at his place and I would wake up early and run to the shower to wash the disgusting bar smell off of my body. I was self-conscious in the mornings, a much more nervous version of the girl I had been the night before. I was shy around him and found myself playing less of a "cool girl" role like I'd done in my other relationships.

Drew didn't wait to call or play the games other guys did. He called every day and we talked on the phone even though we lived just one block away from each other. We would see each other almost every night and I didn't have to wonder if he liked me. He told me he did. Better yet, he showed me by taking me to dinners, movies and brunches.

About a month into dating, Drew invited me to go with him on a family vacation to Myrtle Beach. My immediate thought was, "how am I going to pay for this?"

"I would love to go!" I told him.

I managed to rearrange my schedule to get off work and so that I would be able to spend the week with him. I also needed to call my parents because even though we didn't talk daily, I always let them know where I was.

"Hello." my mom answered.

"Hi Mom. How are you?" I said wondering how I was going to lay this out for her.

"Oh, we're good. What's new with you?" she asked.

"Well, you know last week, when you asked if I had a boyfriend?" I led.

"Yes?" she replied.

"I know I said no, that I didn't. But that was because I wasn't quite sure if this thing was going to pan out, but it turns out that it is, and yes, I have a boyfriend." I stammered.

"Oh?" she said, in a tone that indicated she was wondering what I could possibly be talking about.

"And, we like each other so much so we're going on a little trip together. With his family. I mean, we're going with his family so it's not like just the two of us." I rushed through the rest of the explanation.

At this point in my life I had lived away from my parents for nearly a decade. I was an adult, yet I still felt like I always needed to ask permission. I thought if my parents knew that there were going to be *real* adult supervision they would approve. I still didn't think of myself as grown up.

The trip was amazing. I hardly noticed Drew's family because I was lovesick. We went on long beach walks and told each other stories about our pasts. We went out dancing and he made me breakfast in bed. We met his grandfather, who lived there, and I felt like I had won a VIP pass to the interworking of his life. I was floating on a pink cloud and life had never been so sweet. I was falling in love even though I'd only known him for a short time. I had never felt so happy.

When the trip ended our relationship kept going strong. I often think back to what may have happened if he had left town for a week right as we were starting out. Would I have spent the week going out every night and forget to return his calls? Would he meet someone else or answer a call from an ex leading back into their relationship? The trip sealed our exclusivity and I was now in a real relationship.

I didn't give Drew all of the details about my anxiety. The last thing I wanted to do was be dramatic. A few times, he would reach for my hand and I would have to pull away because it was dripping with sweat. I would mention that my palms were clammy because I felt a bit nervous. Also, the feeling of falling in love had drowned out the feeling of anxiety for a while, so it was almost like I felt better.

Being in a relationship was good for me. It provided me with some stability that I just didn't have when I was alone. I knew that each day I would wake up, go to work and spend the evening with Drew. This meant less going out on weeknights and no more Sunday nights spent drinking at the bar with whoever I could find. I realized how much my life was missing some kind of routine or rhythm.

This stability carried over to other areas of my life. I got promoted at work. I started eating better. I would actually eat meals at home and cook for myself. We heated up a frozen pizza or would make spaghetti sauce and angel hair pasta. It was food a fourth-grader could make, but it somehow made me feel grown up. I began walking at the park or around the block after work. I even went back to the gym where I had been paying a monthly membership for a step aerobics class followed by an ab class. We made smoothies and I learned what organic meant and about superfoods like kale. This new lifestyle thrilled me and I finally felt like I was actually being an adult.

We started staying in instead of going out to bars on the weekends. Drew didn't like wasting money on beers at bars. He preferred to drink at home and avoid the cover charges. This was fine by me because I wanted nothing more than to spend every second with him. I had trouble focusing on anything else. When I was at work, I checked my phone 500 times a day to see if he had called or texted. I daydreamed about seeing him, traveling with him and even marrying him. I didn't care if I ever talked to or saw another person as long as I could be with him. We would just hang out at his nice, clean, quiet home *that he owned* and I was the happiest I had ever been. Before I knew it, we were staying in all the time and drinking while watching movies, drinking while making dinner, and drinking on Wednesdays.

The idea of drinking at home felt scandalous to me. I had never done this and I loved it. It was the equivalent of curling up with a blanket on a cold afternoon. Drinking in the comfort of your own home, wearing your pajamas and having no social expectations was the greatest thing ever. And since we were still going to bed at a reasonable hour and getting up early in the morning, I saw this as responsible. The hangovers weren't nearly as bad. It was shocking how much better I could function the next day if I only drank a few drinks at home and didn't stay out at a bar all night.

Drew and I were happy together. One night, about six months after we had started dating, we were laying on the couch watching a movie. I told him that I had something to tell him. My heart started pounding so hard that I could no longer hear. My hands were dripping with sweat and a little shaky.

I felt as though I might pass out but I carried on and blurted out, "I love you." then waited for what felt like an eternity for him to respond. I knew it was probably too early to be disclosing such a giant emotion. Ironically, this wasn't a word that I threw around. I knew the magnitude of expressing love, but somehow I wasn't at all worried. I thought that Drew loved me too.

I thought that he would immediately respond with something like "Oh thank God, I was just waiting for the right time to say it. I love you so much." I was naively optimistic.

"Thank you." He said as genuine as humanly possible. So genuine, in fact, that at first I mistook it for an "I love you too." He rubbed my hair and we both stared at the movie. I laid there perfectly still and was never more relieved that we weren't facing each other. I am sure that he could have read the disappointment all over my face. I didn't pay attention to a single thing going on as I reviewed what had just happened. I resolved that I didn't care if he didn't love me back because what I felt was true. I was glad that I'd said it. A few months later Drew finally concurred that he did, in fact, love me too.

Eventually, I had to fess up to Drew that I was in credit card debt. We were headed to an Arcade Fire Concert that

I had "paid" for by charging the tickets on a credit card that I had stopped making payments on. On the way, I got another call from the credit card company, informing me that I had missed a payment and now my interest would go up. My minimum payment was now more than my rent and all my bills put together. I cried and told Drew the whole truth. I could tell that he was frustrated and it was a major turn off.

Drew wasn't impulsive and he didn't want anything. He wasn't seduced by cute clothes and the latest CDs. He was well aware of the cost of alcohol and bar hopping and did things like have a few drinks at home before meeting out at a bar to reduce the cost. He was patient with me and helped me come up with ideas to get a loan so that I could get out from under the interest rates of the credit cards. I called my parents and disappointed them (yet again) by asking for some financial help. Before I knew it, I was debt free and my spending habits arrived at a new level of maturity. Meaning that I stopped buying things that I couldn't afford.

One weekend, after we had dated for well over a year, I went out of town to visit family in Chicago. Drew called and told me he had gone to look at a house. It was in one of my favorite neighborhoods in all of Louisville, Kentucky, and it was pretty close to some friends of ours.

"I'm thinking I might buy this house," he told me over the phone.

At first, I felt a pang of jealousy. He was getting ready to buy his second house and I just learned how to buy groceries without charging them to a credit card. He explained the house needed some work, but that he really liked the neighborhood.

"Will you come see it with me as soon as you get back?" he asked.

"Yes, of course" I said thinking how fun it would be if he wanted me to help him decorate.

When I got back to Louisville, we went to look at the house. It was a Tudor style and it was old, as most of the homes in that area. It had a little stained-glass window on the front door and the kitchen had a beautiful built in shelf that was original to the home. It was really big, especially for one person, but Drew was very savvy financially and was probably already thinking about the resale value.

"I want you to live here with me," he said.

"Yes!" I exclaimed as though he had just gotten down on one knee and proposed.

We moved in together. Things started happening fast. Within a few months we got engaged right there in our new home and we spent the next year planning our wedding.

On September 19, 2009 we got married. I was 28 years old. I wore my grandmother's wedding dress, altered from its original style into a long sleeveless gown. It was old and hadn't been preserved all that well so it had a yellowish tint to it. We invited all our family and friends and had our wedding in a small chapel near our home. It felt so special to have our worlds collide all in one place. It would be the only time that these two groups of people would come together at the same time and place and it was glorious. Things had fallen perfectly into place.

Once Drew and I were married, we followed along with all the things we thought we should be doing. We focused on our careers, saved money, went on responsible beach vacations and talked about having children. I even switched from drinking my beloved Bud Light to red wine and microbrews which were locally sourced and better for the environment. Both of those seemed like the right kinds of drinks for home drinking. Beers on the porch, wine with dinner, a glass here, a mug there. Evening or even early afternoon. Anything goes when you are drinking at home.

We took a trip to Wine Country. I had never been to California and immediately fell in love. The weather, the landscape and the vineyards were breathtaking. The dry sun felt so good on my body. We drove up mountains and down through valleys in our rental car, stopping at each winery along the way. We drank red wine, white wine, wine made in cellars, wine made in organic fields. We drank peach wine, and port wine and sparkling wine. We listened to men and women dressed in ties, or wearing cowboy boots, who looked tan and healthy telling us all the facts about the grapes we were drinking.

"This Malbec was made right after World War II." I heard as I stood on one side of a dark mahogany bar, trying to swish my wine around in the glass like the other sophisticated grown-ups.

"Isn't this delicious?" I said to Drew as I felt a warm tingle going down my throat and into my stomach.

We took pictures of the beautiful architecture and the amazing farms that would go on as far as the eye could see. We bought bottle after bottle and even joined a wine subscription. I started liking brie and baguettes and learned what cheeses and breads paired with the wine I bought so that I could serve it correctly once we got back home.

But once we returned to our normal lives, I didn't get to enjoy much of the wine and I never drank a single drop of our six-month subscription. I found out I was pregnant with our first child shortly after our trip.

"Drew!" I screamed from the bathroom holding a positive pregnancy test. My hands were shaking and I felt more shock than excitement.

"It says I'm pregnant!" I said handing him the test with questioning eyes.

He hugged me close. "Are you okay?" he asked.

I was happy, but I suddenly felt like my body had been invaded. The whole concept of pregnancy, which I thought I was prepared for, seemed so scientific and scary. I couldn't quite grasp that there was a baby growing inside my body.

After the initial shock I was happy to be pregnant and excited to take on my new role as mother. I was so nauseous the first three months that I really couldn't fathom the idea of drinking. I would wake up dizzy and have to eat saltine crackers in bed in order to be able to stand up. It felt as if I had spent the night drinking and partying, but I hadn't had a sip. It was a horrible feeling and there were times that I regretted getting pregnant. Once I started feeling a bit better, I began doing some maternal planning. I spent my time thinking about how to decorate the nursery and Googled what car seat was the safest. I also took on a new obsession about natural childbirth.

I spent much of my nine months researching childbirth, particularly the business side of giving birth. My anxiety was growing and it seemed to land here. Now that I was no longer drinking to take the edge off, I was with myself all the time. I wondered if the pregnancy hormones had unlocked the anxiety that I had almost forgotten due to my current stability. The anxiety had been hiding behind love sickness, vacationing, nightly drinks and learning how to become an adult. Regardless, it was back and taking place in the form of childbirth. I learned stats, figures and all about the epidemic of medicated births and c-sections. In my state there was an inexplicable amount of c-sections and medicated births. There were no natural birthing centers and many women I knew opted to schedule a c-section rather than go into labor naturally. I watched a documentary, read books and decided I wanted a natural, unmedicated and vaginal childbirth. I also began to develop an unhealthy mistrust of doctors.

Instead of talking with my doctors about my concerns and asking actual people (instead of internet people) questions about why the stats were so astounding I remained quiet. I made up my mind that my doctors wanted me to have a c-section so that they could "get it over with" and therefore refused to trust them with my fears and uncertainties about giving birth. I tried to control the situation with lies and secrets so that I wouldn't have to face any uncomfortable conversations. I learned later that these were obsessions and the constant thoughts were actually called loop thoughts and were a symptom of Generalized Anxiety Disorder.

"Yes, I'm fine." I would say. "No birth plan here because we will just go with the flow." I lied as I reviewed every detail of the birth plan in my head. I hoped no one could detect the fear in my voice as we talked about what might happen when the time came to give birth. This "paranoia" started to take a physical toll on my body. It was like all of my anxiety about becoming a mother had manifested in this natural childbirth situation. At nearly all of my monthly well checks, as soon as the doctor stepped into my room, I would get lightheaded and pass out. My heart rate would skyrocket and I would start sweating profusely in a full-on panic attack. No one knew this was a panic attack because I didn't mention a word of feeling nervous and the doctors just called it a "weird pregnancy symptom."

I was on my way to one of my final well visits, driving the new four-door sedan that I traded for my fiery red coupe. The car seat was already properly installed in the back, awaiting the baby's first ride. My maternity top was too tight and stretched awkwardly around my belly. I had gained almost 60 pounds and I was the most uncomfortable I had ever been in my life. I had to push my seat back so far that I could barely reach the pedals. As I got closer to my doctor's office, I started to get that feeling again. A darkness would fill my eyes as I got lightheaded and started sweating. It was so bad that I had to pull into the parking lot across from the office in fear that I might pass out behind the wheel. After a few moments I was able to regain my sight, park in the garage and walk into the office. But my heart rate was out of control and my blood pressure was too high. The doctor uttered the words I had feared my entire pregnancy: "I need you to go straight to the hospital to be induced."

I was pissed. It was too late to try to explain the anxiety. To assure everyone it wasn't preeclampsia and that the reason my blood pressure was so high was because I was scared that she was going to knock me out and take my baby. It was too late to go over the facts and to have a rational discussion of my birth plan. There was no time to explain that I hadn't shared this with her before because I have anxiety and I was blacking out at all of our appointments due to stress instead of just some "weird pregnancy symptom."

She explained that my blood pressure was so high that I was at risk for a stroke and the best thing we could do "was get your baby out safely." The words I tried to avoid for nine months. I laid on the table with a bunch of monitors hooked up to my belly and wondered how I would even get my maternity top off in order to give birth. It felt so tight that I assumed I would need to be cut out of it. I couldn't breathe. I couldn't talk.

I nodded yes and agreed to walk through the sky walk corridor to the delivery room. She informed me that I would have plenty of time to call my husband and for him to arrive. She and the nurse walked me to the checkout counter and I nodded that I felt fine and could walk. I somehow managed to get out words of thank you and smile nicely at them as I tried to make sure that they knew I was a good patient. But as I left the office, without even thinking, I walked straight to my car. I called my husband and told him to meet me at home. When he got there, I was bouncing on a birthing ball, begging my baby to start coming. I tried everything in the books to try to induce the labor myself. I even went to see my general practitioner and got my blood pressure taken, explaining that I didn't think I was going to have a stroke but that I had panic attacks every time I went to my OBGYN. My blood pressure was a bit lower, but she kindly touched my arm and told me to go have my baby.

I called my doula, a lady that we had hired to help us maintain the path of natural childbirth, and asked her opinion. I made Drew call the doctor and tell them that we would come in but only for a consultation. They agreed, but when we got to our room it was set up with all kinds of monitors, needles covered in plastic and an IV ready to go. The room smelled like disinfectant and it was freezing cold. The on-call delivery doctor came in and took my blood pressure again.

"Your blood pressure is way too high" she said, staring at me coldly.

"What are my options? Can I do something to lower it?" I said sheepishly, wondering why she seemed so angry with me even though we had just met.

"If you don't get induced, you're at risk for having a *dead baby*." she threatened.

Dead baby? I thought. Did she just say dead baby? How was I supposed to explain myself against that? Of course I didn't want to kill my baby! Now I was second-guessing myself, I felt like my beliefs were extreme. Why was I being so selfish? What was wrong with me? I felt like I had already failed my first task at motherhood.

"Okay, just induce." I caved.

Twelve hours later, the Pitocin did nothing. Not a single contraction, no dilation, no movement from the baby. Nothing. I begged the nurses to take me off the monitors so that I could rest and asked them to remove the IV so that I could eat and drink. I had to wait for the next doctor to arrive. Mid-morning a tall, red headed woman I'd never seen before walked into our room. She had authority and held herself in a way that exuded confidence. She wasn't wearing scrubs or a white coat and instead had on a cute outfit and stylish jewelry. I immediately wished I had brushed my teeth and bought one of those cute birthing robes on Etsy. I felt so gross from a night of no sleep and laying in my own sweat on a plastic covered pillow. I wanted to feel like myself and tell this woman the truth. I wanted to trust her.

She sat down next to me and introduced herself.

"I'm Doctor Shuff." she said.

"What do you want to do here Samantha?" her tone was frank, but not angry or frustrated.

This was the first time throughout this whole pregnancy I had been treated like I might know something. My heart was filled with gratitude, so I told her the whole truth. I explained that I didn't want more labor-inducing drugs and that I would like to try for a natural childbirth. I explained that I wanted to go into labor at home and that I needed to eat and drink in order to gain the strength it would take.

As I talked, she started to remove the monitors and the IV. She motioned to the nurses, who were standing there looking annoyed, to order me a plate of food and to allow me to walk around. She explained that I shouldn't leave the hospital because my blood pressure was too high, but that I could stay on "bed rest" for the next 24 hours to see what happened. I cried tears of joy and thanked her from the bottom of my heart.

For the next 24 hours I meandered around the hospital. Women came in, had their babies and left with a new addition to their family. I watched TV, ate a grilled cheese sandwich and walked back and forth to the water machine to fill my cup. No one talked to me, the nurses didn't check in on me, and I felt like a burden to everyone.

But when my time was up, I could tell that everyone had seen enough. Dr. Stuff returned and briefed me on the plan. She explained the dangers of waiting longer in scientific terms and suggested that it was time to induce labor again and move forward. I trusted her and was also keenly aware that she would only be here for another day before a new doctor's shift. If I wanted her to deliver my baby, I needed to get started. So, I agreed to everything she suggested.

The next 24 hours were brutal. From the massive pain of Pitocin-induced contractions, to finally agreeing to the epidural, to the fear of what was happening to my lower half, my baby boy was finally born.

His face was bruised and swollen from a long, difficult descent and I quickly realized that I should have spent my time learning about being a parent instead of researching stats on c-sections. I was exhausted and in terrible pain, then someone handed me a wounded, crying newborn baby who was having difficulty breathing and asked me to keep him alive.

Everything felt too difficult. I was so overwhelmed I couldn't function. Nursing was impossible, I had trouble soothing his nonstop crying, and the only way I could bear the pain of childbirth was with an IV filled with pain meds. There was a dark cloud hanging over my head that I couldn't escape.

The next three months were more of the same. I was somehow keeping him alive, but it wasn't easy. There were so many people coming around wanting to see him and hold him. There was continuous advice and information giving. Everyone had an opinion, trying to be helpful by telling me what I should do and shouldn't do. It was a parade of gifts of food, adorable baby outfits, guilt and stress.

In between each visit was the agonizing stress of having to feed him. Nursing was the most painful thing I had ever done and I knew something wasn't right, but I had already decided and told the world that I was a nursing mom. So I tried to force us into natural feeding while missing out on opportunities to bond and relish the sweetness of newborn life. I didn't know I could change my mind. I didn't know that I didn't have to do something that was too hard and too painful. I didn't feel supported. I didn't fit into either the nursing or the formula feeding community of moms. I felt alone on an island where everyone spoke a foreign language and I couldn't think straight from sleep deprivation and the constant sound of a crying baby. I began to wonder how bad alcohol was for breast milk. Drinking a couple of good beers seemed to take the edge off and some sources even said that the barley in beer was good for milk production. I even found an article that said, "Best Beers For Breastfeeding Moms." I breathed a sigh of relief. Drinking while breastfeeding wasn't irresponsible, I thought, it was okay and even good.

5

Hangovers for Adults

My friends came over for dinner and drinks one night when my son was about three months old. Sarah and Ben were also expecting a baby in a few months. Sarah was wearing a long maternity dress and glowing that pregnancy glow. The one that I'd had just a few months prior that was now replaced with vomit and milk stains and wrapped in mesh underwear as big as a King-sized comforter. They brought us food and a sweet baby gift and we sat down, poured glasses of wine and told them about what life was like now that we were parents. Sarah and I were very close and I felt that I could be honest about my experience.

The dark circles under my eyes and the manic tone in my voice may have scared her a bit. I told her parenting was hard and that I was pissed off that no one had told me the truth. I told her that between the sleep deprivation and constant worry, being a mom was actually the single most difficult thing I had ever done. I was agitated and my hands may have been shaky as I sipped my glass of wine.

"I'm scared to cook" I said to Sarah, staring right into her eyes.

"What do you mean?" she questioned nervously.

"I'm scared that when I get the knife out of the drawer, I will somehow accidentally stab him." I told her, as serious as a heart attack.

"What if I drop the knife on his head? Or trip and fall on him while he's in the bouncy?" I implored, hoping that she would have a research-based answer with statistics on babies being stabbed accidentally while their mothers chopped garlic.

"Oh." she said, shifting her gaze away from my intense eye contact.

It didn't occur to me that I just told a sweet pregnant, hopeful mom-to-be that I thought I might stab my baby. I shared with her that the nights were long and lonely. That the minute the sun went down, I began to feel the darkest doom come over my body. as I prepared for a night shift of feeding, changing diapers and rocking my colicky baby to sleep. My dear friends left that night with a panic in their eyes, but I was already pacing the floor and manically cleaning up the mess from our dinner. I didn't notice how insane I must have sounded, nor did I care. I had slipped into a funk that I thought all new moms felt.

Drew knew I was struggling, but we were so sleep deprived, we were both really suffering. We both got out of bed in the mornings and left for work on only a few non-consecutive hours of sleep. We were both fueled on adrenaline and confusion.

But Drew didn't have nursing issues and he didn't have to bear the weight of being the mother. For me, being a mom was all encompassing. It didn't matter if I was working, holding the baby, taking a shower, with or without the baby. I was constantly worrying, fretting, concerned and questioning parenting. I don't think Drew felt that way. He cared, loved and tended to the baby but without all the guilt, worry and fear. I tried not to project my feelings onto him.

A few weeks later, another friend had a baby. I was still suffering from the sleepless nights, confusion around my son's nursing issues and the denial that what I was feeling may be post partum depression. I couldn't wait to see my friend's new son. I went to visit and took her a gift basket of food and a sweet baby blanket. As soon as we sat down in the living room, I said to her "Isn't this the worst thing that's ever happened to you?" hoping to finally have someone with whom I could share my misery.

As I looked over, she was staring down at her sweet baby who was sleeping well and not crying and thrashing like my son. She was holding him tight and appeared to be perfectly content sitting all day with him. She looked up at me as if I were crazy. I was mortified and prayed that the meds from her c-section hadn't yet worn off and that she would never remember me saying such an insane thing. That was the day I stopped telling people about how hard parenting was for me.

I lived for the nightly glass of wine. All the moms were doing it. Well, at least that's what those cute little wooden signs in every store said. "They Whine I Wine." "You're The Reason I Drink." "Mommy's Sippy Cup." These slogans were my lifeline. I mean, if people were making hand-painted tea towels about drinking and parenting, then selling them in high end boutiques owned by chic women, how bad could it be? The signs, t-shirts, online memes and hilarious blogs took away any ounce of guilt that I may have associated with carrying a baby in one hand and a wine glass in the other. After all, they were posted by yoga instructors, wellness gurus, celebrities and beautiful and admirable women. I was a mom now and according to business, tv shows, movies, commercials and ads, this is what moms do. We drink. It seemed like the one thing we could all agree on.

I would wake up in the mornings feeling like shit. I didn't know if it was the wine, sleep deprivation, boredom or the anxiety, but I was never refreshed. I dreaded getting out of bed and ready for work. I walked around like a zombie until the caffeine started to make its way through my veins. It was a different kind of hangover. It wasn't the kind that sent me hovering over the toilet like some wild weekends in college. In fact, it was almost impossible to recognize as being alcohol induced. It was a feeling of exhaustion, fogginess, aching bones and a constant hum of anxiety and worry. I could barely tell the difference between feeling hungover or just generally feeling like shit due to parenthood and boring adulthood. I was reminded of a sign that I once saw that said, "Welcome to adulthood, I hope you like Ibuprofen."

I got off work, picked up the baby, came home, started dinner and poured myself the responsible glass of red wine that felt so warm and safe. I no longer thought of alcohol as a party. Instead, I used it to reduce the edge so that I could get through the remainder of the mundane day. I wasn't really getting drunk anymore. Instead, I was making sure that the lovely buzz that made me feel numb stayed with me for the remainder of my day. Since having a baby had limited our ability to go out, have fun and be free. The wine was something to look forward to. Drinking was something to "do." It was my new activity. A reward or an event to take place in the midst of so much sameness.

Meeting a baby's needs was a constant and never-ending task. He was getting older and could sit up on his own. I threw a big blanket on the ground, poured myself a second glass of wine or sometimes third and sat right next to him. Sometimes Drew and I shared a growler (which was like a big pitcher of beer from a brewery). We drank and waited. I knew in no time, he would coo or cry and I would need to jump up to help him with whatever he needed. A bottle, a diaper change, a toy to distract him, a new position to sit in. I predicted his every desire and met it as quickly as possible just like all good moms. It was exhausting, but I told myself that this is what I wanted, so I would need to follow through the best I could.

Most of the other moms I knew seemed to love this job of waiting and responding to their baby's every need. They all seemed to be smiling sweetly at their babies. I felt stiff and unnatural next to them. I would see moms nursing openly with ease or rocking their babies to sleep in their arms. My son's naps and nighttime routine were similar to performing a surgical procedure. We had 300 steps that needed to be executed perfectly. Warm the bottle, rock for five minutes, wrap him up in a blanket cocoon, set the temperature in his room to a perfect seventy degrees, make sure it is pitch dark and turn on the sound machine at just the right level (not too loud and not too quiet).

Then, we had to lie him down in his crib while still holding and shushing. We were required to bend over, still holding him with our bodies half in the crib and half out. Our backs would ache and I would dream of ways that I could detach my arm and leave it there so that I could go to the bathroom or get a drink of water. It felt like years until we could finally pull away, inch by inch, slowly and cautiously. Then we had to tip-toe or sometimes barrel roll out of the room to make sure not to hit that one floorboard that squeaked very loudly. In what felt like less than five seconds, he would wake up rested and ready for us to come get him.

It was a struggle at first for me to let go of control. I really wanted to cope with the unknowns of parenthood with a schedule, a strict routine, a plan. One that would go exactly as I predicted. I wanted him to sleep through the night and take naps at my scheduled naptime. I wanted him to eat the baby food I made with excitement and eagerness. But none of this was his jam. In fact, I was learning that he was anxious too. He also needed control. He wanted to sleep on his schedule and eat foods that felt good in his mouth. He wanted his room to be light and the sound machine off.

We learned together slowly. We each gave up a little control in order to have peace. I let my jaw relax and my arms became less stiff when I held him. I leaned into the times that he didn't want to nap and we rocked and played peekaboo or this little piggy instead. I stopped worrying about how long it would take for him to sleep through the night and allowed myself to enjoy the nighttime snuggles. We started bonding deeply.

As time went on, he started doing more things. I was delighted with each new milestone. When he rolled over for the first time, his first attempts to crawl, when he pointed at things and when mimicked the sign language we taught him for "more" I was overwhelmed with joy. I couldn't believe how proud I was. Even though I was still feeling depressed, I felt this deep aching love for him.

One day I was lying in bed next to him. He was napping and I was staring at him like I often did both out of protection and bliss. By now, he could say a few words like "ite" for "light" and "dog dog" every time we passed by an animal. He was approaching age one. Things were getting easier for me and parenting was becoming sweeter. He was sleeping more and eating solid foods. We had adjusted to the stark transition of being a twosome to a threesome and we were distancing ourselves from our old lives as we grew into our new ones.

My husband walked into our bedroom and sat down on our matted comforter moving the stuffed animals and board books aside.

"Maybe we should have another baby?" he said staring at our sweet sleeping baby boy.

My son was laying there on his back with his arms up over his head. He was sucking on his pacifier with his eyes closed tightly. He looked so peaceful. Every time I paused to look at him my heart would burst open with love. I loved him so much that it ached. I recalled a friend telling me that the love that you have for your child is indescribable. There were no words to describe the depth of my connection to him.

I often read him a book called *I Love You Stinky Face*. The child character asks his mother if she would love him if he turned into things like "a super smelly skunk" or a "slimy swamp monster." The mother responds with reassurance such as, if you were a slimy swamp monster, "I would build a house right next to the swamp and take care of you always. When you splashed to the surface, I would say I love you my little swamp monster." At this moment, I knew I would build a house on a swamp to take care of my son. I would do anything for him.

"Okay." I whispered back to my husband with a grin.

I got pregnant easily and before we knew it, we were expecting our baby girl. At the time, it didn't really occur to me that I still had a baby boy. He seemed so old at his ripe age of one. I assumed that by the time his baby sister was born, he would basically be driving and ordering his own meals at restaurants. They would be two years apart and, though I knew so many people with siblings that were two years older or younger, I had no idea what the logistics of that would be. I was over the medical birth experience and onto more important things like who would take care of our children while we worked.

After hours of research, numbers crunching and the agonizing stress of making adult decisions we decided that I would stay home with the kids. Unfortunately, my job in social work just didn't pay very much money and it didn't make sense to spend my entire paycheck on childcare when the work/life balance was already so hard.

When I agreed to be a stay at home parent, I thought it meant being off work. I had never *not worked* and the thought of this made me so excited. It would be like one long weekend, like a holiday break, a vacation. I couldn't wait!

I planned it all out. I would get so much accomplished. I would meal prep like I had always wanted to do, go to mama and baby classes and learn sign language with the kids. I was going to use cloth diapers since I would have so much time on my hands. I couldn't wait to join a board of directors for a non-profit, volunteer at the shelter and take the kids to visit the elderly.

My daughter was a perfect baby. Her temperament and demeanor were so different from my son right from the start. She completed our family by filling in the pieces that we were all missing. She was very inquisitive and curious about the world. She hadn't decided if she was angry or overjoyed about life. She wasn't trying to fix something right away by crying every time something was unknown. She was present and patient. She slowly took it all in. My bond with her was instant. I wore her in a baby carrier on my chest 24/7. This was out of convenience, so that I could use my hands to change my son's diaper, feed him lunch and help him into his car seat. But also out of a deep connection. We were both content when I wore her. I felt like one of those women in Africa who wear their babies in a cloth on their back while they work outside all day. She was a part of me.

It also helped with the transition. My son didn't realize that his new baby sister was a living and breathing being because he was still a baby himself at just two years old. When he came to meet her in the hospital for the first time, he walked right into the room and said "Hi." very clearly and loudly to the baby before climbing right up into the hospital bed with me showing something that he got from preschool that day. When she was in her carrier on my chest, I could still pick him up after his falls, hold him close and read a book and even put him on my hip at times.

I was blessed to have two healthy children and couldn't have asked for anything more. But within a month of giving birth to my daughter and being home with both children, the reality of my situation sat in. There is no such thing as accomplishment when you have two babies. I spent all day trying to get one of them to sleep. I would clean up the Cheerios just in time for someone to spill more Cheerios. I changed 609 diapers a day. I couldn't find time to take a shower or get dressed because what do you do with two babies when you need to be alone in the bathroom?

Instead of accomplishing I waited. I waited for Drew to come home so that I could "have a minute." I waited for him to bring me wine, or beer and dinner because there's no chance in hell I was making something. I waited to relax, or rest, or shower, or change out of my pajamas, or scream at him for "not helping with the babies." Drinking at 5 pm became as normal as getting a glass of water. It's what we did.

Somehow the boredom and mundane created chaos in my head. I was used to fast paced work with a high level of drama. Sitting around with two nonverbal, bald headed babies all day was the complete opposite of that. My anxiety was suddenly worse than ever before. I would pace the floors until 5 pm and then pour a glass of wine or have a beer or two to try to take some of the edge off, but often it left me feeling tired and groggy the next morning. I hated waking up like that.

I felt this constant need to escape, but there was just no getting out. It was too hard to take the babies' places with the car seats, diapers, nursing, snacks and who knows what else would come up. I couldn't check out with a show or a phone call because the babies would always interrupt with crying or their need for something else.

Drew and I were getting along but he may have been getting tired of my level of intensity by this point. At the end of his long workday, he wanted to come home, relax and play with his adorable babies. But I wanted to give him a play by play of my worries. I filled our discussions with topics like where the kids would go to college. Did you know that some diapers are filled with cancer causing chemicals? How can we be sure to keep their food organic? And, also are we taking steps to remember never to leave the babies in the car when it's hot?

He never got angry, but he may have begun tuning me out, walking away and refusing to engage in my craziness. I'm thankful that he didn't fuel my anxiety by playing into these conversations, but at times, I wanted him to care as much as I did. I wanted him to carry some of this irrational burden so that I could rest. I felt jealous and a little resentful at times. This is when the "itch" began. It was an urge, a buzz, a discomfort that I felt deep inside my body. I couldn't describe it in words, and I didn't know exactly what it meant, but it kept me scratching. I would scratch one place by trying to make a tiny tweak to my life (like walking for exercise) and find that it wasn't there. I would scratch another place by educating myself on things like organic food, but that didn't quite resolve it. I would search high and low for "how to live better" so that I could make the itch go away.

One cold February day my son had turned three and my daughter was approaching age one. I was only thirty-four but felt ninety-five because I was so tired and achy. I actually thought I might suffocate. I was surrounded by loads of plastic baby toys, baskets, music thingys and laundry. So much laundry. I couldn't step anywhere without jamming my toe on something or knocking into a noise making toy that sounded to me like nails down a chalkboard. The house, the sameness and our situation was making me crazy.

I googled "home organization" and came across a website about minimalism. These two guys were suggesting that instead of organizing all of your crap, you should just get rid of it. I was amazed by this remarkable concept. It had never once occurred to me to get rid of things. In fact, I had spent most of my life trying to obtain more.

A switch went off, a spark came through me. I felt like I could finally accomplish something. I became obsessed. I gave the kids a bowl full of snacks to keep them occupied and within a few hours I had read every single one of *The Minimalists* blog posts. I was going through our pantry and throwing out old food that I had never thought to get rid of. I went through our four bedrooms and looked at each closet filled to the brim with clothes, shoes, hats, scarfs, wrapping paper, art supplies, extra dishes, blankets, towels, sheets and more. I was shocked to see our things in this new light and having so much stuff made me feel sick.

A surge of energy moved through my body and I grabbed laundry baskets, bins, garbage bags and anything else I could find and spent the next month getting rid of everything we owned. I sold things online, I gave things away, I donated things here and trashed things there. The purge was so therapeutic. I imagined it must be how people feel after they binge and purge on food. A relief, a sense of calm, an escape of some kind.

We eventually got rid of so much stuff that we no longer had the need for our big house so we decided to move into a much smaller, two-bedroom house, with one bathroom. People thought we were absolutely crazy. We were doing the opposite of what most of our friends were doing, which was upsizing as their family grew. But we knew this move was right for us. I felt like change might help ease my anxiety.

Drew called on me one Friday, my daughter's first birthday, and said he was on his way home early from work. I was surprised that he was leaving work early but excited to get the weekend started. When I hung up the phone, I looked around at the big empty house that we were getting ready to sell. I was so eager to move and get a fresh new start for our lives. An easier, more simple life was exactly what I was looking for. Less clutter, less stress and less chaos.

6

This is Living?

"I got fired." Drew said matter-of-factly as he walked through the door carrying a cardboard box containing all the things from his office.

I stared at the box he was holding. There were three picture frames filled with adorable pictures of the kids. Earlier that year, someone he worked with asked me to print them off for her so that she and other staff could decorate Drew's office for boss's day. Now he was holding them in a cardboard box after being fired. I got lost in my thoughts about how much this looked like all the scenes from TV shows and movies of people getting fired. Characters coming home through their back doors, carrying their box of things that no one really gives a shit about in the first place.

My heart started pounding out of my chest and despite the terrible news I reacted with a big giant smile. He must have been confused by my reaction but he was still so shocked that he didn't say a word.

"What happened?" I asked, already knowing that I

wouldn't be able to listen to the answer because my mind was spinning.

"They said, things just weren't working out." Drew said as he stared off into space as if the answer would be written on the wall behind me.

He was a banker who had worked his way up the corporate ladder. It was a small bank and Drew had found it easy to go from branch manager, to sales manager, to managing the mortgage company. However, as the years went on, he was becoming more and more resentful of corporate life. He was a numbers guru and started making real estate investments on the side. This led to him getting a real estate license and working a side hustle. I guessed that the bank found out about his second job (that he spent time working on during his first job) and decided he was no longer a "good fit."

Although Drew had been unhappy at work, getting fired crushed him. I hid my absolute joy, bubbling with excitement at the thought of him being home to help me with our babies! I knew that we would be okay financially, since we had already downsized, and I was thrilled that he would be home more often.

We sat down in the living room while the kids roamed around, asking us to open this or hold that. I went to the fridge and got out two beers. I popped the tops, relishing the sound of that crisp carbonation as it hit air for the first time. I handed one to Drew to wash away his sorrows and I had the other, taking in each cold sip like a celebration. This was the day I learned that I would no longer be doing this parenting thing alone and I was filled with joy. Screw corporate jobs, big houses and all the rules. I wanted to do life differently.

Turns out, Drew had been itching too. This is why our marriage worked. Neither of us subscribed to the status quo and we were constantly seeking "epic shit" (as Drew would say). For me, this was probably fueled by anxiety and uneasiness. I didn't like staying the same because without constant progression the anxiety would rise. I was able to distract myself by "growing." I felt like a giant tree stump with tons of branches, twisty twigs, hollow parts and dead leaves in places where I left that part of myself behind. In some ways I was innocent and just wanted to know more, see what else was out there, and get a different perspective. I was bored by staying the same.

We moved into our new "tiny" home with only the essentials and our little babies both still in diapers. We started making more real estate investments, working together on real estate projects and spending a ton of time together. At first it was amazing. We were together as a family and coparenting all the time. It felt a lot like vacation. If I wanted to go for a run, I just told Drew and he would be responsible for the kids.

If I wanted to take a shower, Drew was there to keep someone from pulling a bookshelf down on themselves or falling down the basement stairs that didn't yet have a child lock. Soon the kids started asking daddy to open their snacks or hold their hands while they tried a new adventure. Drew would even take the kids places during the day to give me breaks.

As far as our schedule was concerned, we could do whatever we wanted. We would go out for lunches, spend the afternoons at microbreweries, travel and take naps in the middle of the day. We weren't on anyone else's schedule and it was really fun. We drank a lot. I began to wonder if drinking every day was normal. I knew a lot of people who drank every day. And based on my childhood beliefs, there was nothing wrong at all with having a drink or two at happy hour. Most people I knew did this. Sometimes I had two or three drinks at night and on weekends I might have five drinks. Some nights I'd have no drinks. I could go without drinking anytime I wanted. But, honestly, I really didn't do any kind of living without drinking. If I wasn't drinking, I was probably sick, on some kind of diet or cleanse or hung over from too many the night before. It was rare that I would just choose not to drink.

Sometimes I would poll my friends with kids. I would ask, "Do you guys drink every night now that we don't go out anymore?" Most of the time the answer was yes. Not every single night, not too much, but a drink or three seemed to be the norm.

Drew drank, too. He had a few drinks every night and more on the weekends. If we had a babysitter, we would drink like we were in college and get completely hammered. Much of our relationship involved drinking. We went bar-hopping together in the early days, making out on the dance floor after way too many drinks. More recently, we made lists of breweries we visited and beers we loved. We built memories around beer. It was one thing we had in common. The coconut porter from that cute place in Florida. The beautiful brewery in California with the fish-pond and the fried olives. The view of the mountains from our favorite brewery in North Carolina. Some of our greatest times together had been with drinks.

Or had they? Over the years there had been incidents. After our trip to a brewery in Hawaii on our honeymoon, I picked a huge fight because there was no place to dance. I ended up sleeping on the bathroom floor because I couldn't "stand to be in the same room" as him. After the coconut porters and the long night, I was so hungover and shaky for the early flight the next morning that I needed help to make it through airport security.

Then there was the night we were out of town and I

stayed at the bar far too long. I stumbled into the hotel room waking the kids, laughing out loud, falling out of bed and leaving him angry at me for days. And what about that night, a couple months ago, in Colorado where I gave my phone number to a bunch of random people who texted me for days wondering, "if I was coming." Coming where? With who? I had no idea.

I wasn't always drunk, but sometimes I had one or two too many. Enough to leave a bad taste in my mouth, keep me from sleeping well and for me to wake up groggy with a bit of headache. Again, it would have been easy to dismiss these feelings as a hangover. I wasn't swaying over the toilet (except on rare occasions). Instead, I was feeling nervous and edgy, tired and groggy, irritable and snappy. I would ruminate on negative thoughts or obsess about cleaning the house.

I wasn't "partying." There were no late nights, no funny stories, no incidents and literally nothing to talk about the next day. Instead, I drank at happy hour starting at 5 pm while moving through our nightly series of tasks. Dinner, baths, brushing teeth, bedtime stories and bed all while holding a glass or a cold amber bottle. Sometimes we had friends over. Sometimes we walked to a neighborhood restaurant. Sometimes we gathered with family. And most times I was a little bit drunk. Not too drunk. Not "alcoholic" drunk. Not even really noticeably drunk. Just drunk enough to wake up at 3 in the morning with a headache and a pounding chest. Just drunk enough to start sweating the minute my eyes opened with anxiety. Just drunk enough to leave me with a slight hangover that manifested in guilt and shame. I hated feeling this way.

I had been working so hard to manage my anxiety. I was thirty-five years old and I felt like it still wasn't under control. We downsized, we limited our stress, I had recently started running and I loved it. I was reading about natural ways to cope with anxiety and started to implement strategies like deep breathing, doing something calming before bed to help trigger a good night's rest and reading self-help books. Over the years, I had transformed my diet. I ate mostly vegetarian, organic and whole foods that I bought from expensive stores or farmer's markets. I was learning to take my health very seriously and that diet, sleep, exercise were all keys to coping with anxiety and living well. I was really putting more effort toward my mental health and even my physical health. I hated that I woke up feeling a bit off and not my best because of drinking. I always felt guilty for drinking, even if it was just a couple of drinks, because I was trying so hard to "be healthy."

Despite my efforts, my anxiety was back and becoming uncontrollable. The newness of the downsize had worn off. I was having trouble sleeping and would wake up all night long to see what I "heard" or look out the window to see if someone was there. I was so mentally hungover at times that I couldn't do small things like order a pizza or drop a letter off at the post office. I was paranoid and assumed that anyone who saw me would know that I had a hangover.

My anxiety told me all kinds of crazy things that were both terrifying and completely irrational. I spent my days thinking things like I shouldn't send my child to school because there might be a school shooting. Or, I shouldn't go buy diapers at the store because someone could attack me and kidnap the kids. Or, going on a walk isn't safe because we could be hit by cars. Sometimes, it was more insidious than irrational fear. I would wake up in the morning after a cookout or friendly gathering and feel certain that everyone hated me because I talked too loudly. I told myself that my kids needed me and that I wasn't there for them. I told myself that I could have started a fire in the house or left the door unlocked. I told myself that I acted like a fool in front of my friends. I told myself that no one in the whole wide world could possibly understand what I was going through.

I did make an appointment to see my doctor. As I sat in the waiting room my whole body was sweating even though I was freezing. I sat in the cold chair waiting on her to come into the little room with the table covered in paper and the picture of the skeleton on the wall. As I stared at it, I realized that I really didn't know that much about how the body worked and made a mental note to learn more about the human body.

"What brings you in today hon?" she asked as she sat down. She was also the doctor of my children and I had been coming to her since I graduated from college. I had mentioned to her a few times that I was anxious, but told her that I did not want to take meds. She knew that I liked using natural approaches to health, but she didn't know that meant drinking.

"I'm feeling pretty awful. I'm anxious all the time and I am so tired." I said as my voice started to crack.

"What do you think is up?" she asked as she took my blood pressure and asked me to breathe in and out slowly while she listened to my chest with her stethoscope.

"I'm not sure. Could we do some blood tests to see if my iron is low?" I asked.

And that's what we did. My blood work came back normal. She offered for me to try some anti-depressants, saying it might help with my mood and energy, but I was adamant that the side effects were too bad and therefore declined.

I knew I needed help for anxiety. I knew that I couldn't keep up this perfectionism (which by now was borderline obsessive compulsive) as I would find myself putting away things that I had just gotten out to use or washing up our guests' dishes before they were even finished eating. But how? How could I let people in on what was going on? How could I change when I was already so overwhelmed with the one hundred tiny little things that I had to do each day that wiped me of all my energy and zapped me of hope? I knew that drinking was really no longer an appropriate way to manage my symptoms. But how could I stop? I wasn't even an alcoholic.

7

Drinking To Cope

In 2016 the major news was Trump was elected President. My anxiety was getting worse because I was so isolated with the kids. I needed something to focus on other than dirty dishes and putting away books and toys. Social work wasn't really an option for me because the hours were long and the pay was low. I still wanted to be with the kids but just not every single waking moment. They were getting older and a little more manageable. My son was four and my daughter was two.

I talked everything over with Drew and we decided that I should get my real estate license and help with our business. I took real estate classes online while still taking care of both kids. We continued to make real estate investments including an investment at a nearby lake. We bought a little tiny cabin that was so small that the bathroom sink was actually in the bedroom. We got it at a great price, fully furnished and ready to use.

We were so excited to use this cabin and quickly started spending weekends there. We weren't used to life in the country and really enjoyed doing things like chopping wood for the fire and cooking food on the outdoor grill. It was like a mini vacation. We would host friends and family there. Sometimes we would rent a boat at the nearby marina. Lake life was a perfect addition to our lives. The kids could roam freely and safely in the woods which was something that was difficult to do in the city. Our house was on the corner of a busy street and even getting them in the car safely was a challenge back home. We loved it so much that we decided to buy a boat for ourselves so that we could use the water and the cabin as much as possible. It was a great escape.

In order to offset the cost of all of this, we decided that when we weren't using the cabin we could rent it on a short term rental website. The cabin rented so much that we eventually weren't able to use it at all. Drew was great at maximizing opportunity and he saw this as a business. We reserved the cabin for business use only and began building a few more cabins nearby for rental purposes. Managing the cabins became a fulltime job and provided me with a pretty steady income.

I also started to help clients buy houses. I found that I loved working with first time homebuyers and my social work skills were coming in handy. Buying and selling a house was a very stressful process and I felt I actually had the training to help my clients cope emotionally.

I loved having something to do and a focus besides taking care of the kids. I felt like my life had a purpose other than being mom and that was a good thing.

Although I was working, I didn't ever go to an office. I didn't really have coworkers, other than my husband. Unless I was going to home showings, I rarely saw adults regularly. In other words, I was isolated.

I took to social media as a way to be "social." I used Facebook, got the news on my phone, and had access to lots of people's opinions literally at my fingertips. As the election divided everyone into camps, it felt like my social media feed went from friends showing cute pics of their babies to an outright political shit show. My peace loving, hippy "friends" were now engaging in horrible Facebook fights with what appeared to be gun obsessed racists. Wait, weren't these all the same people who sent me that sweet Christmas card last year spreading love and encouragement?

On social media there was a major divide and hate seemed to be oozing out of everyone. Fear took over and everyone retreated to the safety of what they knew. Any kind of disagreement felt like an assault on our freedom and rights and there was no meeting in the middle. The hate talk, the nasty memes, the constant pendulum swing from one side to the other (you either love guns and hate children or love children and hate guns) was the perfect storm for someone with anxiety that always fears the worst. The lack of real social engagement and new obsession with social media kept me on the edge of my seat all day while cortisol surged through my blood.

I would read someone's nasty post and spend the afternoon in a fake argument inside my head with that person telling them how wrong they were and how they needed to reconcile. I would cry as I read through posts from people who I admire and love, wondering how they could possibly agree with the content that they shared. And I would choke with panic every time there was another terrorist attack or school shooting which furthered the divide and strengthened everyone's existing political agenda.

In addition to my social media stress, I also had another thing weighing on me. My son had started kindergarten and I suddenly missed him terribly. I was filled with guilt and remorse for not spending more time with him when I had him in my care the five years prior. I tortured myself with wondering why we didn't have those mommy/son date days that I had pinned from Pinterest or why I never built that fort with him like I had promised. Now he was gone all day and it felt like I was no longer in charge of our family.

My daughter spent the mornings at preschool and now our house was back to quiet. It had been years since I'd had a few hours at a time to myself and I wasn't quite sure what to do. I thought I would love the freedom and do all sorts of creative things with my time, but I couldn't really find my rhythm. Between drop offs and then picking up my daughter at noon there really wasn't that much time. Sometimes I would do laundry and go to the grocery store but other times I would wander around the house feeling lonely and frustrated that I didn't have the energy to get into those big projects or plans I'd said I would do once the kids were in school. What were they again? I wondered.

I was also triggered that, now that my son was in "real" school, I had to adhere to the rules. He couldn't be late. I couldn't just walk into his classroom like I'd been able to do when he was in preschool. I didn't know all of the kids in his class. I had no idea what he ate for lunch or when he went to the bathroom. I was worried that he didn't drink enough water. He couldn't stay home when he was tired or when the weather was nice and we wanted to have a fun day out. We couldn't leave town on Fridays and head to visit our parents.

Our family was now stuck to a school schedule. Our flexible work schedules were no longer a plus. We couldn't go to the Pumpkin Farm on Tuesdays and to the zoo on Fridays. School started at 9am and he got home from the bus at 4 pm Monday through Friday. It was a major adjustment.

Things started to become very mundane. Wake up, take kids to school and preschool, wait for kids to get home from school, make dinner, give baths and go to bed. I didn't like the new schedule and found myself struggling a lot. I wasn't sleeping. The more mundane things were, the more anxious I grew. I felt a rumbling inside me like I might burst from needing excitement or something more. I was unsettled and angry.

Had I been duped? I had done the things that I thought I was supposed to. I got the husband, the house, the job and had enough money. I had two perfect little blonde-haired cuties that I loved so much it hurt. I had stability, clean countertops and a working car that I liked. I could go on vacations, shop for groceries at Whole Foods, go out to nice dinners every once in a while and I had friends. I had done self-help work and learned things that were important for me to be a contributing member of society. I donated money and volunteered. What more could I ask for? And yet, I was missing something and I couldn't quite put my finger on what it was.

I assumed that everyone else was happy. I figured that if people felt like I did that they'd probably be talking about it. People talked about everything. On social media it was non-stop talking, opinions, suggestions, recommendations and ideas, but I didn't see people talking about "feeling edgy." They sometimes talked about stress. Stress of having too much work or stress with taking care of the kids. But their stress didn't seem the same as anxiety. I also saw people sharing stories of severe depression. The kind that causes hospitalizations or intensive treatment. I even saw people talking about addiction. The kind that had such a strong hold that they couldn't go to work without drinking a bottle of wine.

I knew, from my previous experience of working in

mental health, the type of toll that anxiety, depression and addiction could cause. But somehow, during this period of time, I couldn't connect with that. I saw the people suffering from mental illness actually "suffering." They weren't doing well. They struggled to hold jobs, they had been isolated from their loved ones, they had money issues, housing issues and other things that I considered to be far worse than anything I was experiencing.

Not many moms I saw were saying "hey this shit is hard and it never gets any easier." I didn't see women talking openly about their anxiety and how much worse it became after having children. I didn't see people ever saying anything negative about having a hangover or disliking waking up with a dry mouth after only a couple of glasses of wine. In fact, it seemed like drinking was being celebrated more and more.

I felt like alcohol marketing was targeting me. There were wine bottles made to look like little black dresses, cupcakes and skinny stilettos. There were lower calorie beers so that we could still drink while "getting our bodies back" after having kids. There were entire websites dedicated to sharing drink recipes that were low calorie and could fit into any kind of diet. There were vodkas that tasted like marshmallows and wine spritzers that could pass for seltzer water if a mom wanted to drink one at soccer practice.

I felt alone. I assumed that this feeling of exhaustion, boredom, nervousness and ongoing frustration was just life. I had arrived at adulthood and although I was disappointed, I figured there really wasn't much I could do to change that. I should just suck it up and be like everyone else.

One Wednesday, early in September my husband and I decided to have a fun daytime outing. It was one of those beautiful fall days; the air was crisp but it was warm where the sun touched my skin. We went driving around looking at real estate (one of our favorite pastimes) and decided to stop at a new brewery that had just opened. We took our daughter with us and brought along coloring books and baby dolls for her to play with. We ordered chips and guacamole from the local food truck that sat right outside. We took our seats on the patio overlooking the city and I gulped down one of the most delicious $7 IPAs that I'd ever had. Everything about it was wonderful.

A couple of hours and four heavy beers later it was time to get started on "second shift" as I called it. The time when our son came home from school and the afternoon chores started. I dropped off my husband and daughter at home and I walked to the bus stop a couple of blocks down to get my son off the bus. As I walked, I blasted Coldplay through my iPhone. Between my buzz, the freedom and the beautiful weather I felt like I was winning at life. But when I got to the stop, I felt a change come over me. There were other parents there waiting for their children and I felt annoyed that I had to turn off my music and make small talk. I felt a pang of irritability and was already itching to get back home to have a few more beers.

Then it hit me. Here I am drunk at 4 pm on a weekday while I'm picking up my kid from the bus stop. Could the other parents smell the alcohol? Are other parents drunk right now? I began to justify things in my mind. "It's fine because we were supporting a new local brewery." "Everyone does this kind of thing on pretty days." "It's not like it was a dark, creepy, bar where "alcoholics" go to get their fix." I rambled in my mind as my eyes darted back and forth to the other parents questioning what they might be thinking of me.

I tried consoling myself by being proud that I packed

my baby girl organic snacks and made sure that we all had our BPA free canteens to drink water from when we got thirsty. "Wait, did I drink any water?" I thought as I continued to justify this scenario. "It was just a beer with lunch" I said to myself (even though it was past lunchtime and I had every intention of continuing to drink with dinner). The buzz was beginning to wear off and the reality of having to go home and parent both kids while getting dinner ready and doing reading time, bath time, and bedtime were making me feel angry.

My bright boy stepped off the bus and even though I had been missing him so terribly I now felt irritated. He handed me worksheets to look at that made me feel stressed out. He asked me for snacks that I didn't want to make. He interrupted me when I was trying to talk to him. He had an energy that I couldn't match and it annoyed me that he wasn't calmer. This edge made me hate myself. How could I feel this way after feeling so lonely without him just hours before? I was there with him knowing all the things I should be doing and saying. I knew my love for him was enormous and that a big giant hug or a race to our house would have filled me up in ways that I can't explain. I knew that I was so happy that he was home, back in my care, safe and loved. I knew that I could let the worry of if he would be kidnapped or a victim of a terrible crime lift because I was back in charge.

But at the same time, the IPAs had now exhausted me and I felt bloated and groggy. I was in shackles and chains that felt like a heavy weight to carry. The sun was going down, the fun outing was over and I was already feeling a hangover that began with irritability and anxiety. I wondered where was that fleeting feeling of bliss that I'd had when I took those first few sips of that beer? Why didn't it last longer? I knew that any drinking I did from here on out would only make me feel worse but I couldn't stop, or I didn't want to stop. I didn't know which exactly.

I didn't know this yet, but I had diluted my ability to connect to myself, to my family and to my life by pouring ethanol all over everything. I would learn (thanks to Brené Brown) that you can't selectively numb. You can't numb anxiety and still feel joy. When you numb you lessen your ability to feel (and there's actual science behind this). That's good if you don't want to feel anxiety, anger, sadness and other negative feelings but that also means that you won't be able to feel joy, happiness, relief and exhilaration. I was experiencing this in real time. Things that used to be funny seemed "meh." Things that would normally cause a rush of happiness felt like they were happening outside of me. I would think "this is a happy thing that's happening right now" (like one of my kids laughing or running up to hug me after not school) but I really couldn't *feel* the happiness. A favorite song would come on the radio and I couldn't get pumped up about it anymore. I didn't even bother to turn up the volume. Vacations didn't feel all that exciting, delicious meals weren't as satisfying, being outside did nothing for me, even exercise had lost its allure.

The only thing that felt exciting, happy or joyful was the thought of drinking or escaping. I would get pumped as I made my way to the fridge and opened that first cold beer to be paired perfectly with whatever mundane task I was doing. Or, as I poured that first glass of red wine, I would get excited about the fact that soon I would get a little rush of tingling that would make me feel loopy and loose. Alcohol had hijacked my brain making me think that alcohol was the one good thing…but I had no idea. Instead, I thought I was missing was joy. I did have the recipe for happiness according to society but I must have gotten the measurements confused. Maybe I was using the wrong ingredients.

I called my close friend.

"I'm not doing well." I said crying.

"I don't know if it's the fact that school has started or what but I'm so anxious and irritable all the time." I explained while pacing back and forth.

"I feel manic one minute and just exhausted the next. I can't get anything done and I just feel awful." I cried.

She listened carefully and said, "Transition is hard."

She's right, I thought. It's just a transition. I wasn't ready for my baby to start kindergarten and this will all go away once I get used to things. But I knew I was lying to myself; I'd felt this way for a while.

Regardless, I set out looking for joy. I ordered self-help books and made another appointment to see my doctor.

"I just don't feel right." I explained at my appointment.

"Can you check my thyroid?" I asked hoping that she might ask me some more questions about my mental health.

I held out my arm as the tech at my primary care doctor drew blood. There was silence in the room as I choked back tears. I wished she would ask me about my mental health again. I wished that she would ask me how much I had been drinking and give me some kind of guideline for non-alcoholic adulthood drinking. Maybe she knew how much alcohol was too much even if you weren't an alcoholic. She didn't ask. She must have assumed that I may have a thyroid problem. I was well dressed and clean. I used manners and said thank you. I was educated and I brought both of my children to her for the well visits right on time. I never missed an appointment and always arrived early. I had insurance and she knew I had a stable job. I didn't have it in me to tell her that I was falling apart. She had known me for too long and I was embarrassed and ashamed.

My thyroid was fine, so I tried finding joy in healthier recipes. I amped up my physical health regime and I ate spinach smoothies for breakfast and salads for lunch. I made more quinoa and kale. I meal prepped and spent hours searching websites for the right kind of diet for my blood type or my personality or for women with children. No amount of kale made me feel better.

I looked for joy on the weekends as I poured beers down my throat in the name of fun. I went to concerts. In the summer I hung out at friends' pools having drinks. I attended street fairs. I went to mommy wine nights. I went on trips. While there was some short-term relief, I never felt long lasting joy. When the weekend was over and the hangover set in, I was back to feeling anxious and exhausted.

I looked for joy in stores. I redecorated the kids' room and bought proper toy storage. I got a new sundress and a new pair of black jeans. I bought gifts for people and shopped online, hoping that joy that would show up at my doorstep in an Amazon Prime box.

It was useless. Joy was nowhere to be found. And the more that I searched the more depressed I became. I wondered who I thought I was looking for more. I felt selfish for trying to get more happiness. There were people in the world suffering; there were wars, hunger, trauma, poverty, racism and other terrible things in the world and I was seeking to be *happy*. I told myself I didn't need joy and that I was lucky. I had a few beers to help me cope with the guilt.

8

Thank God for Other People's Hangovers

I don't know if it was God, Spirit Guides, the Universe or the CBD oil I was trying, but something kept telling me alcohol was making me sick. Something kept saying "it's the alcohol." So, I would search and become confused. According to some websites, the recommended amount of alcohol for women was no more than one drink per day. I was definitely drinking more than one drink per day, so maybe it was the alcohol. I wondered if maybe I was an alcoholic? But then other websites would go over the criteria for alcoholism. Those sites categorized alcoholics as people who got arrested, passed out during the day and lost their ability to perform daily tasks without drinking. That didn't describe me at all.

This dilemma was agonizing. I drank more than one drink per day, I woke up a little bit hungover at times, I felt foggy a lot and had this nagging hunch that my alcohol consumption was compromising my happiness. On the other hand, I had no symptoms of alcoholism. Where was the diagnosis for the person in between? The gray area drinker? The drinking that causes occasional problems?

Where were the articles and stats on that? Why wasn't there any information out there for people who were in between? There had to be others like me, something between being a happy drinker and sad, desperate alcoholic.

After that terrible day on the lake, I had to find out more. I suspected there was a connection between my drinking and my growing mental illness. I was in unfamiliar territory and it felt scary. The more research I did, I felt I was gaining insight and I might be onto something. It was like there was a secret or something. Something I wasn't meant to discover. The articles I read, the sites I visited, the information out there all had this underlying message that was like *Alcohol is bad, but it's safe for you to keep on drinking. Unless of course you're an alcoholic.*

I started thinking about all the people that I knew in my life. On the rare occasion that I did cross paths with someone who no longer drank, I automatically assumed they had a dark history and were still silently and anonymously wrangling with their demons. I would place that person into the category of "those that can't drink" while I safely stayed in my group of "those who can drink." I felt reassured and maybe even a little relieved when they would confirm my beliefs with a drinking story about something that I hadn't done. Like getting a DUI, or drinking and snorting cocaine or drinking and leaving their kids home alone. I would think to myself *Check! That's it! There it is! There's that thing that they did that makes them different from me. I'm still safe to continue drinking.*

This black and white thinking was harmful. Since, according to Google, I didn't qualify as an "alcoholic" and my experiences led me to believe that you are either an alcoholic or normal drinker. I would stop questioning the alcohol, bury the internal nudge and silence the voices.

Instead, I became resigned to the idea that I had a terrible, unfixable, broken brain.

So, I would go to Whole Foods and buy $274.00 worth of groceries. I would convince myself that my diet was out of control and that I must be eating too many carbs. I would cut, chop, dice and sauté 800 vegetables and eat clean for a week while considering going vegan. Maybe dairy was leading to unhappiness. I would run faster and harder and I would do yoga at night especially mastering the three twisty stretches I learned were for great detoxing. I would listen to podcasts and read books about happiness. I would take detailed notes and reread them to make sure I understood. I would return to my therapy prompts and start doing cognitive behavioral techniques trying to control my anxious thoughts by stopping the cycle. I would swish coconut oil to detox the chemicals from inside my mouth and I would drink apple cider vinegar shots to reduce bloating. I bathed in Epsom salts while eating celery because I read once that the combination of the two could produce good chemicals. I decluttered more and made my home more hygge (a Danish word meaning wellness and contentment in one's home) because it could be that my house wasn't comforting enough. I bought a salt lamp to improve my mood. I swept my floors 22 times a day because I'd heard mess could ignite stress and I didn't want more stress. I controlled, perfected and tweaked all day long adding every intervention from the stacks of magazine articles that told me that doing these things would make me better, heal me, complete me. And, each night, I would drink a few glasses of red wine here or a few beers there. I'd read that red wine was good for you and that beer could help calm my nerves. Then, I woke up and read articles from fitness gurus and health freaks on how to get rid of hangovers.

When nothing seemed to help me feel better, I would revisit the question again. "Am I an Alcoholic?" I would log on to my computer, and click another questionnaire, then slowly and carefully answer.

Has a loved one ever confronted your alcohol use? *No.* Have you been late to work 8 of the last 14 days? *No.* Have you begun drinking before noon? *No—unless of course it's Derby day, or I'm having mimosas at the baby shower, a baseball game or it's Sunday Funday.* Have you experienced marital issues or family arguments over alcohol? *No.* Have you lost friends? *No.* Do you drink alone? *No.*

I never, ever partied anymore. On the rare occasions that I did go out to a bar I never stayed out late. Hell, I went to bed before 10 on most nights so that I could wake up early to work out. I thought I "drank responsibly." I didn't drink and drive. I stayed at home and mostly only drank between the hours of 5 and 9 pm. The hours that everyone called happy. Happy Hour.

Meanwhile, I would daydream about getting a DUI or crashing my car into a tree. If I could do something like that, maybe I could qualify as an alcoholic. I would be understood. Then, I could get some help and I would have an excuse to stop drinking. Or, I would run through scenarios where I could fake a mental health breakdown. I could make some kind of scene or do something crazy like walk naked in the street or run away for a weekend. This way I could get some help and people would understand. Everyone supports people who have breakdowns, right? I knew I couldn't really do that so I continued to walk this tightrope where my anxiety felt as though it might choke me but since I knew how to hold it all together I felt I should. I told myself that I needed to do the nice, quiet, non-dramatic, polite thing which was to not project my issues onto others and not to bother anyone.

To an onlooker, I was crushing it! I knew how to hustle, get it all done, my house was always put together and my kids were well fed. The compliments would come pouring in while I sank deeper and deeper into a hole. I had no idea how to get out. I wasn't sleeping, my thoughts were foggy, I had no focus and I didn't even recognize my body. My face was puffy and blotchy with red spots. The area around my ribcage was swollen and bloated. But, I was running more miles and could squat more weights than ever before.

Each time I drank I would find immediate relief, but soon I would realize that my anxiety actually grew bigger than before. My heart pounded fast and I would sweat out of every single pore in my body. In addition to the anxiety, I felt that without drinking I had no identity. I didn't know of a single thing I liked to do. I didn't have any coping skills. I didn't have any hobbies. And I had the unrealistic idea that drinking added value to my life.

Drinking showed up in every single way. I drank with dinner, with lunch on vacation, at kids' birthday parties, at play dates, at happy hour, at the farmers market and at the breweries that we loved. I drank with the preacher, my grocery store clerk, my parents, my yoga instructor, and even my co-workers. I drank to celebrate, to sulk, to gather, to be alone, when sad, when happy, when excited and when scared. Each season had a drink, a glass and a toast. Each feeling had a recipe. Each milestone needed a celebration; and by celebration I meant a comforting grasp around a familiar elixir that would slither down my throat and ooze into my limbs making me feel light and lovely. Life without a drink in hand seemed impossible. The thing I did was drink. It was my passion, my pleasure and my only pastime.

But very deep down I hated it. I hated thinking about

it. I hated knowing that once I cracked open a drink, I would forgo all the progress I made that day, both physically and emotionally. I hated being hungover. I hated waking up in the middle of the night with a disgusting taste in my mouth. I hated that sometimes I couldn't remember if I had already said something. My hands shook and I felt really depressed after I drank. I hated the time it consumed, between thinking about drinking, buying drinks, making drinks and trying to recover from drinking. Most of all, I hated that I knew drinking was probably the cause of everything wrong in my life. But I didn't know how to stop. What would I even say? "I don't like drinking anymore." Yeah right.

Painfully and privately I continued to search. I wondered, wasn't there anything on Google that could help me? There had to be something out there, someone who knew what I was talking about. Someone else who got more anxious after they drank. Someone who had stopped drinking before they became an alcoholic. Someone who had a problem with drinking and possibly a drinking problem?

The messages were so unclear. I would read articles glamorizing alcohol telling me that it was safe and even healthy. Advertisements for wine and beer were instilled in the fiber of my being reminding that alcohol is fun, beautiful and "what we do." I would see yoga instructors, doctors and other people that I thought of as pinnacles of health drinking wine, having a beer or holding up a glass in celebration. Runners, cyclists, artists, teachers, CEOs, hippies, conservatives, moms—someone from every walk of life seemed to agree that alcohol was good. Who was I to question alcohol? How judgmental and rude of me, I thought. But eventually, this narrative stopped making sense to me. There had to be something in between. My beliefs that there were only drunks and casual drinkers were screaming at me to keep digging, there's more to this story.

In my final act of desperation I typed a sentence into my browser that would forever change my life. I think of it like the scene in National Lampoon's *Christmas Vacation* where the main character, Clark, is trying to turn on the Christmas lights (that he has spent days working on). He has tried everything, but they just don't seem to work. After an angry outburst he gives it one last, best shot. He jams the ends of two strands of lights together in slow motion. Alas, the lights come on in a blinding flash and the heavens sing *Hallelujah*. As I stared at the computer screen, the cursor blinked and I slowly typed out the stupid and vain words *"Cool people who don't drink…"* There she was. I could literally hear the angels signing. My heart rate picked up and my hands started to sweat as I read through her first post, the second, then the third. Her name was Holly Whitikar and I knew she would save my life.

The site was called *Hip Sobriety* and it was about Holly's struggle with addiction and her path to sobriety. Her take on alcohol was different and even though our stories weren't exactly the same I could relate to her. First of all, she was female, she was young and she was living, what appeared to be, an amazingly full life without alcohol. She talked about sobriety in a way that had never occurred to me and she gave facts about what alcohol does to your body. She explained why my anxiety grew after each drink and she suggested that any alcohol was harmful no matter what. She shared that lots of people who struggle with alcohol are not clinically addicted. I started to seriously wonder if alcohol was why I had no joy.

She wrote about sobriety as being a life of freedom versus a punishment. She made it seem cool to not drink.

She said, "it's not a sad consequence, it's a proud choice" to be sober. This seemed remarkable and had never once crossed my mind. She suggested that asking yourself if you're an alcoholic is not the right question. Instead, she advised, ask yourself if alcohol is holding you back from living your best life. That was something I understood *deeply*. Yes, clearly it was.

I always assumed all non-drinkers were white-knuckling it through every day. Every birthday, every wedding reception, every good day at work, celebration, vacation and sunset was now dimmed, watered down, had less joy and less life. I felt sorry that they couldn't drink while I was still able to guzzle booze, experience a massive headache for half of the day and shake with anxiety. I felt sad that they could no longer "live" like I could and thought they must feel so mundane. But, Holly was different. She wasn't sad or disappointed with how her life turned out at all. In fact, she was celebrating!

Each post was so enlightening. The science she shared was mind-blowing. She wrote basic, common sense knowledge of what alcohol is and how it works. It was shocking (and embarrassing) that in my 36 years I had never thought to ask. She explained hangovers. Um, hello. No wonder I felt like shit. She wrote about alcohol marketing and how ideas around alcohol are formed. I thought I was supposed to be drinking. I thought drinking was living. I thought it's what we all did to have fun and to let go. I thought it was totally safe and never once questioned whether the terrible side effects of a hangover were my body's way of eliminating poison. I read and read and read. Post after post, I learned something new that challenged my beliefs around alcohol. Holly combatted my ideas about drinking for fun. She challenged the concept of deprivation and willpower as a means to stop and gave other suggestions like self-love and open mindedness. She suggested books and gave ideas for toolkits. It suddenly became clear to me that I knew nothing about my drug of choice. I had been sucked in and deceived. I was angry, but also awake and alert. I was listening and I wanted to know more.

Within a week, *This Naked Mind: Control Alcohol, Find Freedom, Discover Happiness & Change Your Life* by Annie Grace arrived on my doorstep. It was on Holly's reading list, among a bunch of other books that I ordered right away. I went to my room and didn't return until I read it cover to cover. I was amazed by the facts, the details and data around alcohol. I knew that everything Annie Grace was saying was true and it took no convincing. It wasn't the first time that I had been duped into believing that something was good for me when it was actually not.

A few years prior, before having children, I watched some documentaries about the food industry in our culture. I was shocked to learn about the production of food, specifically meat, and the chemicals that covered most of our crops and soils. I learned that messages like "all natural" and "with real fruit" were marketing techniques. It occurred to me my food shouldn't have to tell me it's food and that these ploys were actually brainwashing me into believing that it was good for me. I was angry by this, so I instantly started to change my diet and reconsider how I bought my food.

This book had a similar story. I learned that the alcohol industry was a massive business. I learned that the amount of marketing money that goes into the business was having an effect on my beliefs. I learned that alcohol is a poison, that it can be deadly and that it's dangerous properties aren't just reserved for killing degenerate folks with piercings and brown paper bags. Alcohol causes cancer (it's directly linked to seven different types), messes with our bodily systems and changes our hormones. It affects our dopamine levels, which numbs joy and other positive feelings. It causes our brains to release adrenaline and cortisol, rewiring our stress responses and making it harder to cope with anxiety. Alcohol also depresses our nervous systems and breaks down our immune systems making us more susceptible to illness. It's more addictive than any other drug on the market, killing 88,000 people per year, with deaths among women rising rapidly. I learned that I had bought into lies and deceit.

Annie Grace also explained the science behind why I had no joy. She went into the nitty gritty details about how alcohol rewires your brain leaving you wanting more alcohol.

She explained "...over time the artificial stimulation your brain receives from drinking makes you neurologically unable to experience the pleasure you once did from everyday activities, such as seeing a friend, reading a book, or even having sex."

This explained why I could no longer feel happy about regular things that made me happy before. It explained why moms make memes about drinking and everyone talks about how happy alcohol makes us. It explains why the first thing we do when we gather socially is reach for our drinks. It suddenly made perfect sense that we are all trying to enhance our experiences so we can feel joy.

Furthermore, like Holly, Annie described herself as happy, fulfilled, free from anxiety, no longer on meds for depression and complete. She didn't talk about treatment, recovery or going to AA. She didn't adhere to any kind of title regarding her "alcohol issues" and instead focused on the brain. She talked about the science behind addiction, how alcohol affects our bodies and her body specifically. Her words exuded peace and joy. I trusted that she was authentic. She put thought, research and so much heart into learning about alcohol. But more than anything, she had what I wanted. She had a life of bliss without alcohol.

Both of these women were tearing down the illusion of alcohol with their writing. They made *not* drinking sound way more awesome than drinking. I was jealous of them. They were replacing the images in my head of the girls in *Dirty Dancing* with the crop tops with images of women having stability and an inner knowing. They were looking way cooler and brighter than the blondes on the beach with beers in their hand. They seemed more authentic and real than the moms pushing me to drink and telling me that I needed to escape.

They encouraged me to stay, to try it, to be curious. They didn't mention abstaining or throwing myself into a life of sobriety but encouraged me to explore the idea of not drinking. They suggested forgetting the term alcoholic and just exploring my relationship with alcohol. They made it seem totally normal to do so. I started to ask myself questions. Could alcohol be having adverse effects? Could drinking be increasing my anxiety? Do I really have a faulty brain? Maybe feeling depressed and anxious wasn't my fault? Maybe adulthood wasn't shitty? Maybe alcohol was to blame and it was holding me back? For the first time, my anger was focused on alcohol and not on myself. I did more research, reading and learning. Soon I was filled with rage. Alcohol wasn't the thing that made life fun. Alcohol wasn't safe. Alcohol wasn't *only* harmful to people with a predisposition to addiction. Alcohol didn't make me cool and witty. Alcohol didn't enhance my connections. Alcohol didn't make me a better dancer. Alcohol didn't take away my anxiety. Alcohol actually causes depression. Alcohol is a bitch!

I started noticing commercials and other advertisements. There were so many about alcohol. They sent the message that alcohol makes sports more fun. Alcohol is for cool people. Alcohol is for beautiful people. There's a beer for that and a wine for this. Why was it that not a single commercial ever showed a drunk person? Not one single commercial or ad demonstrated someone even slightly tipsy from drinking. I had been influenced over my entire life to believe that alcohol was safe, normal and that it would enhance me…and I totally fell for it.

This reminded me of the commercials my kids see for toys. My son begged me for a toy dinosaur that he saw frequently. It's very basic but the children in the ad had placed it in a forest with moving parts and other accessories (that aren't included). My son would see a plastic dinosaur that was in the woods hunting other dinosaurs and toy figures of army men. In the commercial it appeared this dinosaur could run, jump and crush rocks but in real life it was just an immobile piece of junk.

I was like a small child believing everything that the alcohol ads told me. I thought if I drank, I would have more fun. I thought if I held a fancy glass filled with a white bubbly drink, I would be more sophisticated. I thought if I drank a dark heavy beer that I would become moody and unpredictable. I thought if I drank beer made in a sustainable building that I was being ethically responsible. None of this was true.

Day by day I stayed in my room and read. I felt exhausted both from the alcohol withdrawal (that I learned could take at least two weeks and up to a month) and from the massive amount of new information I was taking in. My family thought I was ill. It was as if I had the flu. I would only emerge from my room to get a drink of water and to pee. Actually, it was like someone had died and I was in mourning.

I was mourning the loss of my best friend and my lover. Alcohol was the one relationship that had been with me my entire adult life. It was there for me in good times and in bad. It was the one thing I turned to when I was happy and sad. I would seek it out for every single emotion that I'd ever had. This new information, that it was unsafe, harmful and the cause of my problems made me feel sad, betrayed and terribly lonely.

It felt like finding out that my husband of 20 years had a secret family in the Bahamas. Or, finding out I'd been adopted and my birth parents lived down the street and ran the local grocery store. I was discovering that my beloved, trusted, dependable hobby was a farce. One big fat lie!

I hadn't yet decided that I was going to stop drinking. I was too tired for that. I just happened to not be drinking because I could barely pull myself from bed. I was consumed with reading, deciphering, sleeping and crying.

"Drew, you've got to read this" I said to my husband as he stood at the bedroom door staring at me with both frustration and confusion that I was still wallowing in bed.

"Alcohol is bad. Really bad." I said in a whisper with tears in my eyes.

"Okay." he said uncertainly. Without trying to combat nor confirm the concept.

"I think I've got to take some time off from drinking?" I said in a questioning tone.

I was feeling him out. At first, I thought it would be impossible for me to stop drinking if he were still drinking. Since so much of what we "did" was drink I was worried about how he would feel. Plus, I needed his support.

But Drew was in a different place. He had his own

things going on, his own reckoning with being a human, his own issues to work out. Our relationship worked so well because we made space. He made space for my anxiety but he didn't take it on as his own problem. He supported me, listened and discussed things but he didn't allow it to completely consume our lives. This worked because it led to discomfort for me. I couldn't hide under his protection or allow him to try to take away my issues. These were my problems and he encouraged me to deal however I saw best. I knew I couldn't ask him to stop drinking just because it was no longer working for me.

"I think my anxiety is worse because of alcohol." I explained with very little to no detail.

"I'm going to try to not drink for 21 days." I said before I even knew what that meant.

Looking back, I find it interesting that with all the new information I was learning, the anger I was building toward alcohol and the deep knowing I felt about how bad it was for me, that I was still, in that moment, only willing to commit to not drinking for 21 days.

I think I was terrified of telling people. I had no idea what I would say. I couldn't go and share this new-found information and try to rally them to all stop with me. I couldn't go shoving my opinions on them. This was heavy, deep and personal. So I decided that telling my husband I was taking a break from alcohol for 21 days would buy me time, make more sense and allow me to figure it all out. My desire to please people and to make everything feel okay for everyone else far outweighed my desire to save my own life.

Twenty-one days? Where did I get that figure? Wasn't there a movie with Sandra Bullock about going to rehab for 21 days and then being cured? I googled how long it took to break a habit and the consensus was 21 days.

It seemed like a lifetime. Other than when I was pregnant, I hadn't gone more than three days without a drink in more than 15 years. I didn't yet know how I was going to do this. I didn't have a plan but I had a deep understanding. I didn't have to be an alcoholic to stop drinking. I could explore my relationship with alcohol just like most people explore their relationship with things like sugar and gluten. I could be someone who had personal issues with alcohol that didn't have to meet some kind of number or consequence. I could be someone who just decides to stop drinking. This was a massive mind shift.

As I pulled myself out of bed and passed by my bedroom mirror, I saw someone. I saw a stranger wrapped up in an oversized sweatshirt that was wrinkled from laying too long. I saw matted hair that needed to be washed. I saw a girl who looked weak, tired and defeated. She looked like she was suffering. But she knew something. She knew change was coming.

9

No Thank You Please

The first person (aside from my husband) that I told I wasn't drinking was the cashier at Trader Joe's. I'd had nothing but happy and successful conversations with every single cashier when shopping there. They were always filled with positivity and encouragement asking me about my day or sharing a cooking hack for that new item I was trying. I always walked away with a smile.

"How's your day going?" the perky guy in the TJ Hawaiian shirt asked.

I was about one week into life without alcohol and still wasn't sure exactly what was happening. It was the longest period of time I had gone without a drink (on purpose) in years. I felt as though I had climbed Mount Everest or hiked the Appalachian trail. I was excited and proud.

"Well, I stopped drinking alcohol about a week ago, so there's that." I said, as I felt my face turn beet red and immediately regretted telling him.

My usual self-doubt sat in. I mean a week without a drink was nothing. I knew that. Anyone could go a week without drinking. In fact, most normal people went every week without drinking. Why did I think this was some big accomplishment? This was nothing to be proud of and I suddenly knew that I should be embarrassed and not boastful.

"Oh right on! So cool!" TJ guy said with a level of enthusiasm that felt completely authentic.

A rush of relief came over me as I smiled.

"Yeah, it is cool. Thanks"

Over the next few weeks, I slowly started mentioning to people that I wasn't drinking. I told my running partner during our weekly run that I had gone 11 days without drinking and I was going to try to do 21. I didn't go into too much detail and she was so sweet and encouraging.

I told my best friend that my anxiety was out of control and I had to change something. She already knew I was struggling with my mental health and was very supportive. I told my extended family that I read a book that suggested that alcohol "wasn't that great" for you and so I was taking "some time off" drinking. I told my friend from high school that I was blacking a few times too many (like that day on the lake) and so I gave up alcohol. I told jokes about it. I followed it up with a "for now" or softened it by adding the word "break." I blamed it on depression and anxiety.

I obsessed about what I would say and would lay awake at night thinking up things to tell people when they asked me if I wanted a drink. I said some of the most embarrassing things during this time and turned a nice offer from hosts into horribly awkward moments. Drew and I went to a mutual friend's birthday party when I was newly sober and terrified.

"Can I get you anything to drink?" our host asked.

"Um, no thank you. I'm not drinking right now. I mean I might drink again, but for now, I'm just not. It's not like I was an alcoholic or anything. I'm not an alcoholic. I took some online tests but I never went to a doctor. No thank you. Please." I would say as my voice got weak and I knew that I'd said too much.

"Okay." the host would say with a half-smile, wondering what the hell I was talking about.

Especially since she meant water or tea.

Sometimes, I was let down. I had developed a plan for what I would say when someone asked me why I wasn't drinking. I had prepared, rehearsed and even stressed about how to respond. Then the time would come where I was sure all time would stop and everyone would focus on why I wasn't drinking, but it never came. It appeared most people didn't give a shit if I drank. They didn't give a shit about why I stopped or what happened to me. It seemed like they were focused on their own set of issues, probably making up scenes and preparing for responses to something that I have no intention on asking them about. This was a lightbulb moment.

Sometimes I was very clear with people that I did not think of myself as an alcoholic. Other times I thought I was being clear, but people just assumed. I didn't combat this. I realized that I wasn't the only person who grew up believing that you were either a drinker or a drunk. I realized that this is how most of our culture in the United States views alcohol. Alcohol is either a problem or it's not and there is not really much in between. I hated this thinking and blamed this view, in part, for why I didn't stop drinking sooner.

Those first 21 days were a shit show. I felt so raw. It was as if I were walking around without skin. I had never been to a social engagement, never made it through a happy hour or a dinner party without at least *one* glass of wine or one beer. I had never hung out with friends or been on a boat, to a game, to a concert, a wedding, a funeral or done anything without my best friend booze.

Feeling my anxiety for 21 straight days with no breaks was hard. Very hard. I had always been able to check out, even if it was for just a little bit. I knew no matter how bad things felt, at 5 pm, I would have some kind of relief, however brief. I was an emotional mess. I slept a lot. I laid in bed all the time. I paced the floors worrying about things that were out of my control. Global warming, terrorist attacks, childhood hunger, spousal abuse and more. I walked away from the kids when they talked to me. They were ages five and three and they could be alone for a few minutes watching a show, eating a snack or entertaining themselves for a bit.

I cried a ton. Commercials, Facebook stories, someone saying something insensitive, thinking of things I did and said drunk, would all send me to tears. I felt like I was back in college going through a breakup. I was down in the dumps. I had lost my best friend and this time I couldn't turn to alcohol for help.

But I held steady. I did what my author friends told me to. I implemented different types of "interventions" and began to explore life without alcohol. I started by approaching not drinking with self-love. Instead of punishing myself like I had a million times before, I loved myself through every minute of not drinking for those first few weeks. I allowed myself to feel so sad. I allowed myself to feel scared without an immediate plan to resolve anything. I allowed myself to wallow, eat as much food as I wanted and say no to everything that I didn't want to do (despite my crippling fear that I would end up with absolutely no friends at all).

I was grieving. I missed alcohol terribly and I didn't know how to do life without it. I didn't know where to sit or what to say at social gatherings. I felt horribly awkward and like I had lost my "edge." I didn't feel funny. I felt tired from standing and wondered how I stood at bars for all those years for hours on end.

I was so worried about what people would think of me. I desperately wanted to make my not drinking "okay" for everyone else by ensuring that I wouldn't change a bit. I didn't want to disappoint people. I didn't want to let anyone down. I thought that if I stopped drinking I would devastate my friendships and ruin our good time! I just didn't know how to do something different from the crowd. I didn't want to be isolated, the odd man out. I didn't want anything to change. But that's not all true, I did want things to change, just without any weird social interactions. I wanted it to be easier. I wished for a blanket statement I could tell people like, "I'm an Alcoholic" even though that wasn't exactly true.

I committed to "not drinking right now" and that was as far as I would let myself go. That was my mantra and I said it more than 100 times a day. I knew that when I started down the road of what I would do at the upcoming event, wedding, party, holiday or onset of sad news, I couldn't fathom getting through it sans alcohol. So I stuck with "not right now" through every single moment. At 5 pm I would start saying out loud "look at me, I'm not drinking right now." Same with 5:01 and 5:02 and in the beginning I said it for three straight hours. It helped me be very present and not get too far ahead of myself.

I stretched my body. I had been holding it so tight for years. Abs in, butt clenched, jaw closed, toes curled. I thought if I exhaled or let it go things would completely fall apart. I finally allowed myself to unfurl. I did a downward dog. I sat cross legged with my palms up. I inhaled and exhaled in my nose and out of my mouth. Instead of trying to get out of my body, I leaned into it. I listened to what it said and asked it questions. I wouldn't exactly call it meditating at first, but I stopped fighting off my body and began to allow room for feelings to flow through instead of attaching to my every fiber and allowing them to hold me down like dead weight.

I opened my mind to spirituality.

Over the years, I had grown irritable with organized religion. It seemed like I always felt worse after going to church. I grew up Catholic, but when I decided to have our wedding in a chapel, performed by one of Drew's close family friends (not a priest), I was no longer able to receive communion. I had broken the rule that, in order for the Catholic church to acknowledge my marriage, it must be blessed by a Catholic priest and there must be communion. That stung a bit and seemed like a good time to start trying out new churches. But every time we visited a new place, I struggled to find that feeling of home.

Instead, the author Gabby Bernstein spoke to me. She was my new preacher, priest, pastor and spiritual guru. She had mantras, and prayers, and taught me how to seek guidance from the Universe, or God, or whatever you like to call it. She spoke about connection to all other humans, connection to the Earth and connection to yourself. I consumed her work, her talks, and her books like biscuits dripping with butter. I started to view the world differently. I could see miracles in everyday moments, like my children smiling. I could find snippets of joy. I began to feel worthy.

I would remind myself that being drunk is not a privilege. Holly Whitaker once said "It is not a privilege to drink. It is not a benefit, not a lucky thing, not a talent. It is a privilege to discover you cannot drink, cannot tolerate poison, cannot do that to your body or your mind or your spirit without consequence." I chose to believe her and thought back to the last 10 times I drank. All turning out to be a letdown. All leaving me feeling sick both emotionally and physically. Each time amping up my anxiety and emptying my happiness.

I built up a sobriety toolbox full of "replacement behaviors" when I wanted a drink. At 5 pm I drank peppermint tea and treated myself to any and all desserts (which would later become a problem). I took baths. I got really interested in essential oils and started using lavender, cedarwood and frankincense to calm my nerves and help me sleep. I would concoct oil blends for my diffuser in the same way my husband concocted a moscow mule. I went for walks.

I entered my house a different way, so that the first thing I saw wasn't the fridge and the limes sitting on my kitchen counter. I went to my bedroom to watch movies because there wasn't a side table there for me to set a drink on. I stopped sitting outside in "my chair" because that was where I always drank. I watched YouTube videos and learned to play the ukulele and spent hours obsessing on how to play certain chords. I completely disrupted my general routine because I knew I couldn't sit through my exact same ways and expect not to want a drink.

I drank fizzy water for the first time. I would pack my purse full of LaCroix and Topo Chico. One night, I was at a neighborhood party and I took a purse full of LaCroix with me. I noticed how I held the can, took sips at every pause in conversation, pulled on the napkin that I wrapped around to wipe the condensation. I realized that I used the can as a shield against social anxiety. I drank close to six La Croixs that night and my mind was blown at the way I'd behaved with those cans.

"Oh that's so funny!" I said to a neighbor with a chug.

"I'm doing great. How are you?" chug, chug, chug.

"Yes, he just started kindergarten this year." I told someone I'd just met about my son. Chug, chug, chug, chug.

Hand up to my mouth, hand down on the table. Hand up to my mouth, hand down in front of my waist. I had these little tics, tendencies and rituals that I hadn't ever noticed. I had been using my beer bottles, beer cans and wine glasses as security blankets.

I didn't feel safe without my shield. So for those first few weeks I didn't leave the house without something to hold. I knew that alcohol had taken over my body physically and emotionally, but I was shocked to also see how much I depended on it behaviorally.

All of these "interventions" were working. A couple of weeks went by and I was living my life without alcohol. I found myself noticing the colors of the leaves going from green to yellow and suddenly I could hear the birds singing outside. When I ran, instead of berating myself for what I had drunk the night before, I found that joy washed over my body and I would sometimes be moved to tears. At night, when I put the kids to bed, I would feel overcome with gratitude for being there with them instead of trying to rush them to sleep so I could get back to my drink. I would stare at their sweet faces for as long as I could without wanting anything more in the moment. When I woke up in the mornings, at first, I would feel a rush of panic followed by sheer relief as I realized I wasn't hungover. I didn't have to wonder what I said or did the night before.

There were times I felt like having a drink. Five o'clock, Saturdays, social gatherings and eating out, but day by day my anxiety was improving. I noticed that I could go hours without feeling panicky and I was able to look people in the eye. I could take the kids to the zoo without the fear that I might be attacked. There were even times I would forget I had anxiety at all. This began to outweigh the desire for a drink. I was surprised that things were going so well. While it wasn't always easy, my whole approach just felt so much more positive. It was so different from what I thought it would be: white-knuckling, drooling over alcohol, living a life of deprivation.

I thought back to an event that happened several years ago. I was doing a "clean eating challenge" which meant no alcohol. I was drinking daily during this time, but assumed since I wasn't an alcoholic it must be my diet that was causing my weight gain, depression and overall lethargy. It was summer and I was at the pool with the kids. We were standing in line at the concession stand to get them an ice cream cone and I overheard a woman behind me talking on the phone.

"Oh, I can't wait!" she said.

"I'm going to finish up here, grab a shower and I'll meet you there. We can have drinks first and then go to dinner," she said loudly to the person on the other end of the phone.

I remember feeling so incredibly jealous. Rage came over my body and my heart started to pound. I was so angry that she was "having fun" while I was doing a miserable cleanse. I told myself that I would suck it up for 10 days, use willpower, sacrifice, give up and all the other yucky words.

During that cleanse I didn't replace any of my old habits. I literally stared at the clock from 5 to 9 pm with my tummy rumbling feeling angry and deprived. I cancelled plans, didn't see friends and avoided being in public at all costs so I wouldn't feel tempted to eat normal food or drink. I had the idea that since I had been "bad" by eating terribly I would punish myself with this cleanse to get things back on track. "Back on track" in that case meant a body weight that felt fine enough to look myself in the mirror again. I had no intentions of maintaining this new lifestyle and I planned to go back to being able to drink as much as I wanted and to eat like shit until the cycle repeated itself. This is what I assumed sobriety was like, a punishment for drinking too much. Unsurprisingly, the "challenge" didn't last for the whole 10 days. I was too miserable.

Now, with the help of Holly, Annie Grace, Gabby (and a bunch of new authors that I added to the list like Laura McKowen, Glennon Doyle, Brene Brown and others) I was not thinking about sobriety the same way I had in the past. I explored alcohol through different eyes. I was willing to let go of some of my old beliefs and I was open to being wrong. I looked below the surface and beyond those first five minutes (which were really the only good ones left) of relief I felt once I had a drink in my hand. I had to go deep to realize what drinking actually looked and felt like for me.

It felt gross, heavy and hard. I was consumed with guilt. After drink number one, my mind was filled with constant turbulence. I would spend whatever was left of the night thinking, "Should I have another even though I said only one tonight?" And then justifying each new drink with "This is fine because…" "It's not that much." "We are all getting drunk." Until I reached the point of being numb, which by then meant a terrible hangover was next.

This constant internal banter had become exhausting and overwhelming. I had no room for other thoughts, ideas or creativity of any kind. I was stuck in a constant loop of excuses and no matter what path I chose I would be sure to fail pushing me deeper and deeper into resentment.

Now, I was focused on the things that I was gaining by

not drinking. It felt so freeing to not have to think about drinking. I was also free of headaches, irrational thoughts, loss of sleep, chunks of nights that I can't get back. I was free from worrying if I had too many, or too few, or if I was getting too drunk, or if I was having enough fun, or what the ABV was, or if I ate enough dinner or if I was going to be sick the next day.

Instead of putting all of my energy into what I was losing I now seemed to have this massive room to grow. One of my favorite sober influencers Carly Benson writes, "The act of being alcohol free is much more than not drinking. It's an act of establishing true freedom. You don't just become free from alcohol, you become free from the illusion that you needed it." This was slowly but surely becoming my truth.

During this time I never went to a single AA meeting. I wasn't sure I belonged since I didn't believe myself to be an alcoholic. I was desperate for sober people though. I could only talk to my husband about this newfound passion so much before he got sick of hearing it (and he wasn't sober). I was dying to tell someone in person all of the things I had learned. I wanted to meet with sober people who would bash alcohol with me and talk about how stupid we were for believing the lies. I wanted to talk about how awake I was now and ask them if they felt the same. I wanted to address the mommy wine culture and go on and on about what kind of damage it causes. I wanted to attack commercials, ads and the thousands of innuendos that I was no longer oblivious to and discuss how to fight the system.

I had my books and Holly's blog and I knew they were there for me, but a local, sober, non-AA community wasn't all that easy to come by. I was slowly learning that, just like all belief systems, sobriety had many different layers. It seemed that most sober people did the 12 steps and that almost all of the community surrounding those people thought that the 12 steps were the only way. In some conversations, it felt as though maybe I was doing sober wrong (which is impossible) or that maybe I should just be quiet about the fact that I stopped drinking by using books, essential oils and fizzy water. I thought, I must have it too easy.

There was no great "service" for people like me. It seemed that outside of the couple of books I read that AA was the only path to sobriety. I was frustrated by this at first, because I felt like people rolled their eyes at me when I admitted that I was alcohol free without AA. I believed that the 12 steps were amazing at helping some people heal alcoholism and lots of other mental health issues. But I also believed there were probably lots of ways to stop drinking and wished there were more options available for people like me. As a newly sober person though, I wasn't quite sure how to navigate all of it.

I began to wonder if maybe I shouldn't tell people that I don't drink. My worries started to come back and I worried that my privileged situation might hurt people. My life was so easy in comparison to others and it felt like I was robbing the word "sober" from the people who really deserved the title. I didn't have a rock bottom and therefore I wondered if I should just hide all of this away. But something kept nagging at me.

When the 21 days came to an end I decided to just keep going. I never made a "grand proclamation" that I was going to live a sober life. I didn't tell that to myself or to anyone else. I just kept with my mantra, "I'm not drinking right now." I had already seen so many positive changes. I loved not being hungover. I didn't want to go back to that.

There were still struggles. I remember going out to dinner with some girlfriends

"Can I get you something to drink?" the waiter asked.

"No thank you." I said.

"Are you sure? A glass of red wine or a mojito?"

"Um, no thank you." I said politely but felt annoyed.

"Okay, well I'll just leave this with you in case you change your mind" the waiter said as he slipped me the wine and beer menu.

This same scenario repeated itself on a daily basis. I was now fully aware of the push of alcohol in this culture. People tried to serve me alcohol everywhere I went. There was no safe place. Work meetings, baby showers, yoga classes, farmers market, church and the list goes on. Alcohol was everywhere and there was no way to escape.

I remember wishing that my drug of choice had been cocaine. At least I could quit that without being scorned and pressured to use all of the time. No one would hand over a razor blade and some white powder at restaurants in case I "changed my mind" and wanted to snort some lines later. No one would be giving me the side eye or wish that I would just continue to get high around them instead being lame.

It made me think about smoking, something that I did heavily during college and for a few years after. No one was annoyed with me when I quit smoking. No one was disappointed that I no longer reeked of smoke and had to leave our conversation every 10 minutes to go outside and smoke. No one thought to themselves *"God, I wish she'd just start smoking again."* No one was confused when I quit or asked me if I was pregnant. No one ever jumped to the conclusion that I was a smokaholic every time I said, "I've got to quit smoking." No one judged me for not using the patch or the gum and for going it cold turkey. Everyone knew smoking was bad.

This angered me but gave me more motivation. Each and every scenario where someone would suggest that I drink confirmed what Annie and Holly were talking about as true. Alcohol was an illusion. I had paired drinking with whatever feeling I was seeking in the moment. When I wanted to feel like a cool eccentric chick who loved to buy local, I'd drink IPAs from unheard of local breweries. When I wanted to feel sophisticated and grown up, I'd drink red wine. When I wanted to think of myself as free and airy, I'd drink champagne. When it was daytime, I drank white wine. When I wanted to be rebellious, I drank dark and heavy beer.

I continued to use my tools and my mental health kept improving. I made it through the holidays without drinking, which was a huge milestone. I packed a purse full of fizzy water and pastries and spent most of my time around the food table stuffing my face in an effort to be busy with something. I also escaped to the bathroom quite a bit just to breathe and remind myself that "I'm just not drinking right now."

When Spring rolled around, I was 6 months alcohol free and I'd lost 10 pounds with zero change to my diet or exercise regime. The red blotches on my skin went away. I was sleeping the way that sleep was meant to be—restful, cleansing and beneficial to the next day. My anxiety had improved so much that I could order pizza without feeling nervous and I could look people in the eye when I talked to them. By summer I was 10 months alcohol free and seeing everything differently. It was as if I had been asleep to my life. I was completely numb to it all. Alcohol was diminishing my ability to feel anything.

One day I was at home with the kids and the doorbell

rang. I went to the door without even thinking twice. A man was standing there

"Would you like to support my cause?" he said, handing me some kind of flyer about kids or hunger. I wasn't sure exactly.

"Um, no thanks," I said, closing the door behind me and going on about my day.

This was a turning point. I didn't stand at the window and make up stories about how this man was a burglar and was trying to assess my house in order to rob me later while I slept. I had things under control. My thoughts were less irrational, fewer loops, more fleeting. I didn't spend hours perseverating on things that were completely out of my control. I wasn't paralyzed by fear. I had begun to consider my irrational thoughts like wild monkeys that got in my face yelling gibberish. I ignored, pivoted, walked away.

The correlation between my anxiety being worsened by alcohol was undeniable. This knowledge was powerful and I felt proud.

"People have got to know about this!" I told Drew with a level of enthusiasm I hadn't felt in years.

"Do people know that alcohol makes anxiety worse?" I asked him.

He stared at me blankly as he had done for the past year while I paced back and forth demanding that he know about my newfound research. Drew was still drinking, but he was learning too. He may not have decided to stop drinking all together but he wasn't denying the science either. He read the books, he knew the harm and he was now starting to connect some of the outcomes (for example, having increased anxiety after too many drinks).

"I know so many moms with anxiety who are seeing all of these jokes about how alcohol makes everything go away and now I know it actually makes things so much worse." I continued to say to no one as Drew had walked out of the room.

"I've got to tell them." I said.

The more my anxiety healed the less I cared about using the word sober. My entire adult life had been blanketed with the dark cloud of anxiety. I had tried hundreds of things to try to ease the horrible symptoms. Therapy, medication, exercise and diets. I'd sacrificed thousands of hours of sleep, been too distracted to connect to my loved ones and experienced feelings of terror during the most mundane times. I took advice from health experts, wellness gurus, fitness "pathblazers" and even doctors who had never once mentioned that alcohol was bad for me. In fact, they taught me how and what to drink in order to minimize the hangover and keep feeling my best. They suggested busting my ass with workouts, diet plans, vitamins, organic foods only and natural sleep aids so that I could reward myself with that much needed glass of Rosé or beer at the cookout. These messages were so confusing but I loved them and I wanted them to be right so I didn't have to face the fact that alcohol increases anxiety. I clung to them and I was so happy when the articles were shared, when the jokes were made about us all "needing" alcohol, and when at the end of all of the suggested interventions it was "still okay to drink."

Living without alcohol healed my anxiety. It closed the open wound, only leaving a tiny scar that I would always have but now could easily manage. I had the right to be sober and the less time I spent drinking the more confidence I gained.

10

A Writer Emerges

On September 17, 2017, I hit one year of sobriety. I have never in my life been prouder of anything. Up to this point I had never stuck with anything really. I had always started big plans but struggled to follow through. I could easily be persuaded and I am extremely impulsive. I couldn't believe I had denied alcohol for an entire year!

I woke up eagerly awaiting the reward that I thought would come from going 365 days without drinking. I wondered if it would be divine intervention from the Universe in the form of pure clarity and peace. I wondered if my eyes would sparkle more and if I would have a glowing halo atop my head at all times. I sat close to my phone awaiting phone calls and texts from people who in no way would have known my anniversary date. I wondered if Drew had bought me flowers and secretly planned a babysitter so we could go out on the town and celebrate.

I wasn't a member of AA which means I couldn't go and get a one year chip from a meeting. I considered buying myself some kind of sobriety brooch. I even thought about getting a tattoo.

As the day unfolded, I realized that being one year sober was similar to being seven months and six days sober. It was another day that I wasn't drinking and, while that was a great success, my kids still needed breakfast, I still got work emails and there were still errands to run. I wasn't going to be riding away on a unicorn of bliss.

I thought one year sober was going to mean some kind of closure. But what I learned was that sobriety had made room for other things to rise to the surface. Sobriety made room for me to start living.

Nevertheless, I felt very proud and decided that I could celebrate by sharing. I posted a little blurb about being alcohol free on Facebook for those who I hadn't yet hit with my awkward explanation of why I no longer drank. The response was enormous. People I hadn't talked to in years, hadn't ever talked to, didn't know all that well and close friends for ages reached out to me. I had an outpouring of support and love and, surprisingly, an outpouring of questions and curiosity.

"How much did you drink?" a friend I hadn't seen in ages asked.

"How bad was your anxiety?" moms from the kids' preschool wondered.

"What did your husband say?" strangers questioned.

"Did you go to AA?" others cautioned.

Drew also got an outpouring of support. People were messaging him letting him know that they were there for him and could help out if needed.

While I was so happy for the support there was something telling me that people needed more information. My friends, other moms I knew, Drew's friends and even our families were deserving to know more about my story, our story, the story of alcohol. During conversations about my sobriety, it always felt as if people didn't believe me. No matter what I said, it still seemed that people were unsure. The story that I drank too much, my anxiety was bad and that I "chose" to stop drinking without some kind of consequence or rock bottom didn't make sense. It felt like people either thought I was lying, or they thought I was being dramatic and that they "spilled more" than I drank.

One week in early fall of 2018 I had the kids to myself while Drew was out of town. Both kids were in school and I had a lot of time on my hands. As I moved through the motions of my day, I would spend the day "writing" in my head.

The first story was my thank you note to Holly. When I ran, showered, brushed my teeth, picked up the mail, threw in the laundry and drove in the car I would recite the words I wanted to say to her. "Dear Holly, Thank you. Thank you for saving my life. I wasn't dying of alcohol but I was dying of complacency. Your words and your willingness to share your story…" I would go on and on and found myself lying awake in the middle of the night…writing?

I loved words. When I wrote thank you notes to the kids' teachers, I always got positive feedback on how thoughtful and well-written they were. I also dabbled in blogging a bit. Back in 2010, I wrote a blog called *Dear God…It's Me A Vegetarian*. I told stories about the recipes I cooked as a vegetarian. I wrote and wrote, but I only ever shared this with a few people. Regardless of how irrelevant the blog was, I worked on it as though it were as important as being the CEO of a Fortune 500 company. I took pictures, developed recipes and then got lost as I wrote stories about my life. But once my son was born I had less time for writing on my hands. Then, a few years after the kids were born, I started another blog called *The Year of No Complaints*. It was supposed to be about my quest to go one year without complaining, but it turns out that I couldn't go a single day without complaints. I closed it down and never told a soul.

The second story I told myself every waking moment since I'd posted on Facebook that I'd been sober for a year, was the story of the last time I drank. The one in the first chapter of this book. Then one day, finding myself in a quiet house, I sat down and actually wrote out the story. As the words came from my head, to my fingers, to the white blank page I felt healed. It was so therapeutic to be telling the truth, getting it all out, and being honest about how I drank. I hadn't felt that good in a long time and I liked it. I even felt a little sad when I finished the piece and would go back and reread it over and over again. I called Drew and read it to him and told him I wanted to share it with people. He, like always, was supportive but couldn't have known what I meant by "share it."

Over the next few months, I continued to write stories on a word document on my computer. I wrote about my anxiety. I wrote about struggles with social settings. I wrote about my faulty beliefs. I wrote about being a mom. I wrote about drinking. Before I knew it, I had a lot of "material" and I felt I needed a place to put it. I logged into a blog hosting site and signed up for the basic package. I got a domain name and found a format that I liked. I spent hours and hours converting all of the writing on the word document into a blog format. Each story was a new post that I would "save" but not "publish." I spent hours rewriting, editing and tweaking my stories. I fantasized about actually publishing a story or two and even went on to come up with a name for the site. I called the blog Alive AF (Alcohol Free). When I thought about my journey from that first post to the place that I'm in now the word Alive kept coming up.

All along I thought drinking was living. I believed drinking gave me an edge, made me cool and made my experiences more epic, rich, fun and worthwhile. What experiences exactly? The concert I couldn't remember? The girl's weekend when I puked? The lake days where I couldn't open my own damn eyes because the sun was too bright? Nothing about those experiences made me more alive. Day by day as the chemicals wore off and my body healed, I felt like I was coming back to life.

Life was becoming sweeter. Everyday things were becoming more noticeable. There were times I felt like I was just born into the world. Things I would never notice because I would have been too occupied with crazy thoughts in my head were suddenly apparent. The kids saying something cute would make me genuinely giggle. The love I felt when I spent time with my husband would come rushing to me. I cried tears of joy as we headed back on the lake for the first time sober as if I'd never seen water before. When I heard music, I felt it pulsing through my veins and I would find myself swaying back and forth or sporadically dancing. I was falling in love with myself and with my family all over again.

My mind was so blown by the ordinary and mundane that I had to write about it. Writing was healing me in ways that I could have never predicted. Getting thoughts on the page eased my stress and seemed to make things clear.

I hired a photographer to take pictures of me so that I could put them on the blog. I was so meek when she came to my house, a mom from school that I had just met. I wasn't exactly sure how to explain to her what I was doing. I asked her to take pictures of me and my books, me and my fizzy water, and me and my essential oils. When I explained to her that I was going to write a blog called Alive AF about my journey to living alcohol free I started to cry. Was I being self-absorbed? Was this attention seeking? I didn't even know if I was going to publish this thing, and here I was paying a professional to take pictures of me. I thought maybe I was going crazy.

"I've never done anything like this before. I think I want to write a blog about living my life alcohol free." I said with tears welling up in my eyes.

"That's so cool." she said while adjusting her settings and checking the lighting.

"I'm not trying to be a famous blogger or anything, I'm just hoping that maybe my story can help someone." I explained.

"And, if I'm going to do it, I just want it to look professional." I said more to myself than her, as sweat stains started to form under my armpits.

I remembered this quote by Marianne Williamson, "Our deepest fear is not that we are inadequate. Our deepest fear is that we are powerful beyond measure. It is our light, not our darkness, that most frightens us." Had I been scared of stepping into myself and speaking the truth? Had I hidden behind my anxiety?

One early morning I woke up super restless. It was 4 am and I got out of bed and crept into the living room careful not to make the old floors squeak and wake the kids. The room was pitch dark, the only light glowing from my computer screen. I logged into my blog and looked through all of the hard work that I put in. The pictures, the words and the books. I told myself that starting a blog was stupid. There were eight billion blogs in the world and no one would care about my very boring, mundane, basic story of sobriety.

My heart started pounding and I had tears welling up in my eyes. I had been working so hard on this blog, but I didn't have the guts to put these stories out there for the world. What would my parents think? My friends? My real estate clients? These words, these stories were too personal and I felt incredibly vulnerable. My hands started to shake and scrolled my cursor to the bottom of the first post, the one I pined over for the weeks and read to Drew over the phone. The story of the last time I drank alcohol. I got to action buttons where my choice was "delete" or "save and publish." Before I knew what I was doing, I double clicked publish. Then I shared the post to my Facebook page and slammed my computer shut.

I must have gotten one hundred messages that day. People commented on the post, texted me, messaged me via Facebook and even called me. The blog became a gateway to the community of sober people I was seeking. My blog posts became a conversation starter and people would reach out to me. Some were friends, others were strangers, but people were interested in hearing about my story. Maybe because it wasn't much of a story at all. I looked and behaved like a "normal person." I wasn't showing up drunk at the kids preschool and I wasn't hiding my drinking. My "normal drinking" was much like everyone else's. This sparked some curiosity.

A few readers started to question their relationship with alcohol. They, too, ordered the books, read them, and had an eye-opening experience. Other readers asked to meet with me and wanted to know the inner workings of my life.

"How do you handle holidays and birthday parties?" one reader asked.

I explained my exact process.

"I take bubbly water and I talk to myself about my

experience." I explained. "If I'm having fun, I say it out loud and allow myself to feel what it feels like to have fun without being impaired (which by the way is so much better than "having fun" while impaired)." I went on.

"If I'm not having fun, I take note and realize that maybe I don't like doing this kind of thing anymore. Then I stop doing it. I leave. I walk out. I do all kinds of crazy things for myself that I would have never felt empowered to do had I still been under the curse of alcohol."

"Really?" the reader would ask.

"Really. Trust me." I would assure.

Some readers, however, felt uncomfortable reading my story. While so many they could relate to having too much to drink and feeling hungover, people were still skeptical. Where was the part of my story where I went to a treatment facility? For those who were in recovery (via a program like AA) they assumed that it was unsafe for me to talk about getting sober without doing the 12 steps. Regular drinkers assumed that I just didn't want to be hungover and so I "gave up" alcohol. They figured that I could drink again anytime I wanted.

These assumptions furthered my desire to keep writing. I considered myself one of "nine out of ten" people who have a problem with alcohol but didn't meet the criteria of being clinically addicted. I wondered how many other people were in that category? Maybe they would be interested in hearing more about the role alcohol plays in life in general—not just the role in severe addiction.

I kept searching for sober people and soon I found myself having coffee with strangers in my community who were also working to change the stigma about alcohol. I met Jesse, the founder of the Mocktail Project, a nonprofit working toward inclusion for non-drinkers. He was serving up epic drinks in cocktail glasses so that anyone, anywhere who wished to not imbibe could still feel like part of the party. We quickly became friends and soon I was attending sober events at bars serving only mocktails.

I began reaching out to health practitioners in my community. I wanted to speak to anyone that was talking about holistic health but might be forgetting to mention the important role of alcohol. I wondered how many medical professionals' opinions were formed in the same way as mine and if they were looking at the data. Did doctors and therapists have honest discussions about how much their patients drank? Were they reminding them of the recommendation that safe consumption is less than three drinks per week? If so, why weren't we seeing warnings about all of the effects alcohol has before you become addicted? I've seen an abundance of warnings regarding high fructose corn syrup, the damage that carbs cause and how red meat increases risk factors for heart disease. I can't get online for one minute without being bombarded with the idea that I should go keto, buy all organic, use natural face cleansers and fast as much as possible. Everyone is on board that cocaine is bad and that opioids are a problem. There's an all-out war on gluten! These warnings are probably the reason I took those things seriously and made so many changes to my diet over the years. Warnings are why I don't snort cocaine and why I monitor my kids screen time. Why aren't we talking about alcohol too? Who was benefiting from this?

I continued writing on the blog and with each post my confidence grew. I began to feel empowered to write openly about some of the cultural barriers around drinking. That meant bringing to light difficult concepts. I wrote about the "drug epidemic" and how alcohol isn't included as being dangerous. I wrote about slogans and advertisements for drinking and reminded people that if one, does in fact, "Rosé All Day" they are likely to end up sick, hungover, with a scraped knee and a lost purse.

I wrote about the absolute insanity of mommy drinking culture and how sick I am of moms advertising alcohol as the thing that "gets us through" parenting. I wrote that there is nothing funny about parenting your kid while you're drunk and that we, as women, must stop perpetuating this story that we are too weak to parent without the use of a deadly chemical.

Each time I wrote, fear set in and my ego would tell me that I was playing with fire. My head would fill with self-doubt that my words might hurt people, that I was maybe wrong about things, that I had no writing degree, met no criteria and hadn't received the right permission to write about these subjects. I worried I might hurt people's feelings or that someone might misunderstand my intentions. I even worried that people would call me a hypocrite and think I was self-righteous. But after each post someone would reach out. Someone would thank me and tell me that they, too, had those thoughts. Someone would share a post and just write "This." as their caption. I didn't need the validation that what I was writing was good but I did like knowing that someone could relate.

I liked shining light onto the things that other people may be feeling. I liked letting people know that they weren't alone and that I felt those things too. I liked talking about alcohol in ways that I'd never heard before. And, I liked writing. I loved it, actually. Before I knew it, I outgrew the life that I was clinging to so hard, the life that I was terrified would go away, the beer drinking fun girl life that had engulfed my entire identity. It became a life that I wouldn't wish on my worst enemy.

Don't get me wrong. There were some good times.

There were beautiful memories. There were weddings, and celebrations, and stories of youth that can never be replaced. But those things didn't go away when I stopped drinking. Those things all remain. In sobriety, you get to keep all the love. Not only do you keep it but it comes in very clear. I only removed the bad. The hangxiety, sleep deprivation, dry mouth and the lies that life is only good if I'm in some way altered from my reality. Reality is the gift. Choosing to be sober led me to my purpose. It led me back to my love for writing. It led me to new friends, it strengthened my bond with old friends. It led me to living my life with arms wide open, eagerly awaiting the next thing I can do to change, push myself and to feel awake and alert to my life.

As I write this I'm still healing. I'm over three years sober and there is still so much work to do. I have decided to live my life with purpose and by doing that I've eliminated the choice of the "easy way out." I've chosen to stay. Stay with the pain, the hard times, the anxious thoughts, the sad news. But by choosing to stay I have learned that I can now fully experience the sweet things too. I can stay with happiness, the laughter of my children, the slow sips of my morning coffee and the overwhelming joy that washes over my body at least once a day. My Barre3 instructor once said that "difficulty is a sign of bravery." I don't leave when things get difficult for me anymore. Now I stay.

On a trip to California, I finished the most amazing hike with my husband and eight-year-old son. It was very hard and started uphill, with rocks, switchbacks and desert heat. Several times, my son asked how much longer. From where we were at the bottom, the destination looked like it could take years. Step by step we just kept going. There was no option to turn back and each step brought us closer to our goal. When we got to the top the views were amazing!

My son said, "This is so cool!"

"I know. I'm so glad we kept going." I replied, feeling overly emotional as I do now with many adventures.

"Me too, mom!" he said with a giant smile.

People at the top gave him high fives and told him what a good job he did.

"Do you feel proud?" I asked.

"Yes." He said as he took in the beautiful mountain views.

"Do you think you would feel as proud or excited if you took an elevator up here?" I asked.

"No way!" he said.

"I know exactly what you mean." I smiled as we made our way back down the giant mountain.

11

Alive AF

Throughout my 20s on Sundays I would catch a ride down the road that I currently live on. I was usually headed to the bar where I left my car since I was too drunk to drive home. I would have to go back in, wearing the same clothes from the night before, in the light of day. The place smelled like beer covered washcloths and urine and I would usually gag as I headed to the counter to recover my credit card and close out my tab (feeling shocked at the amount of money I spent on liquid). On my way home I remember feeling a pit in my stomach of shame and guilt as I passed people running, eating in the cute restaurants, walking their dogs or visiting one of the amazing parks in the area.

It wasn't so much that I was ashamed of the shenanigans I had engaged in the night before, but more that I was wasting a day that I could be living. Even back then, as a young 20 something, I sensed that the night life wasn't for me. I yearned for connection, comfort and having control over my days. I wanted to wake up early and go to the farmer's market. I wanted to eat fresh pastries and drink coffee in a coffee shop. I wanted to go for a walk or pop into a cute boutique. I wanted to go to bookstores and spend time dragging my fingers across the titles, slipping a book from the shelf and reading a few pages, pondering. I didn't want to spend my days sleeping, hungover and eating terrible food in a dark, smoke-filled apartment.

As I write this today is Sunday and I am almost three years alcohol free. I woke up early without a dry mouth or a headache. I meditated this morning for 10 minutes and I'm still a work in progress (which I've learned is the whole point).

The guide on my meditation quoted Einstein today, saying, "There are only two ways to live your life. One is as though nothing is a miracle. The other is as though everything is a miracle." I smiled because these are the kinds of messages that I hear daily now. The books I read, the movies I watch, the songs that I've listened to for years are all telling me to be fully awake to this moment of my life. Ironically, I'd never once heard a message like this before sobriety. Next, I read something from an inspirational passage and every word seemed like it was written exactly for me on this particular day and time. I drank my coffee slowly and rubbed my children's sleepy heads as they awoke. I made myself a piece of sourdough cinnamon toast (a recipe that I've loved since I was a teenager) and was delighted by how yummy it tasted. I felt gratitude that I no longer starve myself in the mornings because of what I drank the night before. My hands weren't shaky as I cooked and my stomach didn't feel even the slightest bit queasy. I got dressed, put on my running shoes, grabbed my ear pods, and went for an epic run down that same road where I used to do the walk of shame. I passed by dog walkers, people strolling to church and I could smell bacon and biscuits from a nearby brunch restaurant. I thought to myself, "maybe I'll take the kids there for breakfast later." I smiled a lot.

This is the life that I dreamed of. There's nothing extravagant or fancy about it and yet it is filled with the joy that I was missing for so long.

When I was drinking, I was in a constant state of stress. I spent my days waiting to "take the edge off" creeping that happy hour time up and up regularly. I can remember times when I would hear a good song on the radio and think to myself "next time I'm drinking and having fun I'll play this song." Or, I would fantasize about "having fun" at happy hour. I would spend all day yearning for 5 pm so that I could "relax." While drinking, I was putting off everything about my life until I had a drink in hand. I thought it wouldn't be good enough without the alcohol. Those sober moments felt unworthy of being noticed and so I just passed them all by until the next time I could drink.

Now, when I drive the kids to school in the mornings, I will blare dance music and the kids and I sing at the top of our lungs and dance around in our seats. I relax whenever I feel the need with a good book and cup of something warm and nourishing. Happy Hour is every hour and any hour and sometimes that means a fizzy drink with a squeeze of lime or a walk with a favorite song. It's so empowering and freeing to not have to wait until the weekend or a certain time on the clock to be fully alive.

Today, I have full control (the thing I was always chasing). I know that I can trust myself and that brings so much confidence. I do things now that I would never have done before. I speak up for things that I believe are important. I have compassion for others and myself. I have more patience with myself and my children. I don't have panic attacks and my anxiety is managed by coming back to my breath.

I made a very tiny choice to step away and see what would happen if I stopped drinking. I no longer have to believe the illusion that my life is better with a beer in my hand. I don't have to pack the cooler full of drinks for our road trip or outing. I don't have to think that my Italian dinner would have been better with a glass of Merlot. I don't have to buy into the idea that life is only good if I'm in some way chemically altered. I don't have to buy hangover pills. I don't have to spend hours planning for my hangovers and running through the logistics that will give me time to stave them off. I don't have to wait for happy hour. I don't have to be the anxious girl who stays quiet about her struggles to not make anyone uncomfortable. I don't have to be the stressed-out mom who drinks a little too much at night and then laughs about it by buying a tea towel that says, "they whine I wine."

I am most free from the illusion…not the drink. I can't describe with words how good that feels. Choosing to stop drinking alcohol was the first step that I made toward creating a new life. Not consuming a poisonous liquid was really an insignificant change. Not drinking became about unlearning. I had to unlearn the images, the ideas, the messages, and the innuendos that alcohol gave me life. I had to unlearn my ideas around who is affected by alcohol and learn that there aren't just three types of non-drinkers. There are millions of people who are experiencing their own set of side effects and who are having to make decisions about how alcohol is affecting their life. This unlearning made way for so many other questions. What else could I be wrong about? What else do I have opinions about that could be based on bias, my own personal upbringing, and messaging from the media? As I write this,

I'll likely unlearn some of the things I hold true in this story. I am wide open to understanding that when I know better, I will do better.

Turns out, I didn't need those hangover pills. The cure to my hangover was never a miracle drug, a fitness program, antioxidants or kale. The cure to never having a hangover was always as simple as not drinking. The single thing that will guarantee that I will wake up in the morning fresh, without regret, with my memory intact, and without an overload of anxiety is to just not drink from the bottle. The cure was insanely easy, free and wildly misunderstood.

Conclusion

I finished the first draft of this book in mid March of 2020. The world shut down due to the Coronavirus pandemic and everything changed. At first, the shutdown felt eerily familiar. It felt a lot like the beginning days of sobriety. The not knowing, the isolation and fearing the worst were all things I felt those first few weeks living alcohol free. Much like not drinking, I was without my most beloved coping skills. Group exercise, coffee meetings with other sober people, in-person life coaching and spending time with friends and family halted immediately. Not to mention I was again with my children 24/7 parenting in isolation (the thing that brought me down the first time). But because of my path to sobriety, I knew I could get through this. My ability to adapt, change and accept struggles is so much stronger due to being sober. I've always known that if I can choose not to drink in a culture that begs me to "just give in" every single day, I can do anything. I knew I would get through this pandemic.

Yet here I am, now nine months into the pandemic

Conclusion

with cases rising sharply, no opening of schools in sight and still there's so much unknown. During this time of peace and quiet the world has slowly watched the footage of the murders of George Floyd and Breonna Taylor, an intense election has again divided the country into two stark teams and alcohol use seems to have increased (at least that's what everyone is saying on social media with "hilarious" memes about alcohol being the only thing getting them through life right now). This all feels like a repeat of what I went through just a few years ago.

I'm not gonna lie, the weight of it all has been heavy but somehow I've been able to cope. I didn't have to pace in front of the door to my problems wondering if I should go in. This time I knew to just open the door. I faced (and am still facing) my fears around racism with education. I set boundaries regarding politics. I stopped using social media as a way to check out of my life. I have a whole big bag of coping skills that I rely on—like writing.

I'm just so thankful that I didn't have to face a single second of this year hungover, filled with hangxiety, irrational thoughts and feeling more depressed than necessary. The overload of sorrow for what has been and what is to come is hard, but due to sobriety, I know for sure I can handle this. It's not just not drinking. It's the skills I had to learn, the mindset, the tools. Sobriety is the infrastructure that I lean on when the walls start to crumble.

If you're thinking "but how" I understand. I know how hard it is to see the possibility of living any other way. I really do. But if you have a tug or a pull then maybe stop and listen. The questioning, the listening, the awareness are such wonderful (and way underestimated) first steps. This book isn't meant to provide you with a guide to stop drinking. There are some really great books that already do

Conclusion

that. This book is meant to tell you that you're not alone. Never in the history of ever are you the only person who has looked at their life and wanted something different. My story is the one about the girl you know that gets it. I root for you.

References

Benson, C. (n.d.). *Miracles Are Brewing.* Accessed May 2018 through http://www.miraclesarebrewing.com/blog/page/2/

Bernstein, G. (2014). *May Cause Miracles, A 40 Day Guidebook of Subtle Shifts for Radical Change and Unlimited Happiness* (1st edition). Harmony.

Brown, B. (2010). *The Gifts of Imperfection: Let Go of Who You Think You're Supposed to Be and Embrace Who You Are.* (1st Edition). Hazelden

Doyle, G. (2016). *Love Warrior, A Memoir* (1st Edition). Flatiron Books.

Grace, A. (2015). *This Naked Mind: Control Alcohol, Find Freedom, Discover Happiness & Change Your Life. (*1st Edition*).* Avery:Quill Pen Editorial Services.

Mccour, L. (2003). *I Love You Stinky Face.* Scholastic; Cartwheel Books.

McKowen, L. (2020). *We Are The Luckiest, The Life Changing Magic of a Sober Life.* (1st edition). New World Library.

Millburn and Nicodemus. (n.d.). *The Minimalists.* Accessed

References

January 2014 through https://www.theminimalists.com/archives/#all

Whitikar, H. (2014). *Hip Sobriety*. Accessed September 2017 through https://www.hipsobriety.com/home

Whitikar, H. (2019). *Quit Like a Woman: The Radical Choice to Not Drink in a Culture Obsessed with Alcohol* (1st edition). The Dial Press.

Williamson, M. (1992). *A Return To Love, Reflections on the Principles of A Course In Miracles* (1st Edition). Harper Collins

Acknowledgments

First and foremost I thank Holly Whitaker. Had she not been willing to write up a blog and share it for strangers on the internet my life right now would look completely different. I thank Annie Grace for writing about her story and backing it with facts and information. I want to thank my children who sat next to me, at my feet or near me while I wrote every single word of this book. To Drew, who encouraged me and supported me through both this book and in all of my life. To my parents who have loved me and always given me the "go ahead" to be exactly who I am despite it sometimes being different from them. To my friends for accepting me just as I am which happens to be everchanging. To Anna David, my writing coach who not only taught me everything I know about writing but who is a lovely person that I will forever feel grateful to know. To my writing group, I'm so thankful to know you and to have had the luxury of doing this alongside you all. To my editor, Becky Sasso for helping make sense of all of this. You're a miracle worker! To Onur Askoy, cover designer, for being patient and creating an epic cover. Thank you to

Davis Perkins and Swan Huntley for developmental edits. To the readers of my blog, thank you for being so loyal. You inspire me to keep going in all the times I've felt like giving up. To Authors everywhere, you make my world go round. Thank you.

About the Author

Samantha Perkins had a long and complicated relationship with her anxiety. Despite many different types of interventions, she couldn't quite free herself from the ruminating thoughts, sweaty hands, and the feeling of panic with no apparent trigger whatsoever. That is until she decided to take a long hard look at her alcohol consumption. Once Samantha became alcohol free she was finally able to manage her lifelong issues with anxiety.

Samantha writes about this process on her blog called Alive AF (Alcohol Free). She covers everything from parenting, mental health, relationships, and more while documenting the role that alcohol plays into our everyday lives.

Samantha hosts wellness retreats, leads on online sober bookclub, and helps women (especially mothers) rethink their relationship with alcohol. Samantha has BA in psychology from the University of Kentucky and had a 10 year career in community mental health before transitioning into real estate and now writing.

Find her at:

spaliveaf.com
Instagram.com/samanthaperkins_aliveaf
samanthaperkins30@gmail.com

Made in the USA
Monee, IL
04 January 2021